THE POVERTY
OF EDUCATION

THE POVERTY
OF EDUCATION

A Study in the Politics of Opportunity

DAVID BYRNE, BILL WILLIAMSON
and BARBARA FLETCHER

with a Foreword by J. W. B. Douglas

MARTIN ROBERTSON

First published in 1975 by Martin Robertson and Company Ltd., 17 Quick Street, London N1 8HL.

ISBN 0 85520 072 3 (case edition)
ISBN 0 85520 071 5 (paperback edition)

Printed in Britain at The Pitman Press, Bath.

FOREWORD

THIS is an important study of inequality in educational provision in Britain today. It is in essence an essay on the epidemiology of education using methods similar to those that have been well tried in the study, for example, of local variations in infant mortality. It draws its strength, however, from a penetrating and critical analysis of the current preoccupation with the social determinants of educability and the pessimism which the tendency to 'personalize' educational failure has engendered.

Educational attainment levels of children of equivalent social backgrounds vary according to the region of the country in which they live – and the authors suspect that place of residence may be a more important predictive variable for achievement than the 'educability' measures that are commonly used.

The presence of local differences in educational provision has been frequently noted in the past but dismissed as irrelevant to the general understanding of inequalities in achievement. Thus in 1957 the Ministry of Education (List 69 (1957)) argued that some difference in the local provision of selective schools ' . . . is likely to be fully justified for a number of reasons including the following:

(a) The average level of academic ability may vary from one area to another.

(b) There may be differences in the children's interests or other differences in local circumstances.

(c) Pupils attending independent and direct grant schools whose parents pay any part of the tuition fees are not included. The proportion of these varies from area to area . . .

(d) The figures . . . cannot do justice to the wide variety of provision . . . in Secondary Schools, and in particular to the greatly expanded provision of extended courses in Secondary Modern Schools. Such courses may well correspond to courses in Grammar or Technical Schools in other areas . . . '

The inference from these assertions was that local differences in selective school provision (ranging at that time from 10.5% in Dudley to 53.4% in Caernarvonshire) did not represent maldistribution of educational resources. This was not however the conclusion reached when these assertions were examined in a national sample of children born in 1946. Indeed geographical inequalities in the provision of selective school places accounted for approximately half the social inequalities in selection *after* taking account of the ability and attainment of the children. In areas where provision was good social inequalities were small, in areas where provision was poor inequalities were large. Later studies of the same group have shown that local differences in provision play an increasingly important role in determining and maintaining social inequalities in the secondary and tertiary stages of education.

This, the most important finding of the 1946 study, was ignored in the subsequent debate which was focussed on the secondary issues of home circumstance, parental interest and the need to 'extend our understanding of the actual process whereby a child in a particular home comes to achieve or fail to achieve in school'. It is therefore a pleasure for me to welcome, ten years later, a book which is concerned with the extent to which wastage rates in education are the .predictable outcome of the structure and operation of the educational system at local levels.

It is also timely that the authors should question the currently accepted interpretation of social inequalities in educational achievement as reflecting differences in behaviour and attitudes rather than the relation between classes in society. When social inequalities are equated with inequalities in local educational provision the competition between classes cannot fail to be seen.

The study of local policies and provision, as the authors realise, offers no easy or direct answer to the outstanding questions on educational inequality and the wastage of ability. The description of individual authorities given in chapter 5 shows the complexity of the local circumstances that need to be studied and at the same time provides convincing evidence of the importance of the local educational climate and the past history of local educational policy and provision. Even within individual authorities resources are far from equally shared between schools of the same type or between areas. The available official statistics can only give a superficial and inadequate account of the geographical inequalities that exist and it is good to hear that the authors intend to make intensive studies of individual education areas. In the meantime they have established the necessity of adding a further dimension to studies of educational inequality, so that we will have to look at the spatial distribution of resources as well as at the character- istics of the schools and the attributes of the pupils and their families.

October 1974   *J. W. B. Douglas*

CONTENTS

Foreword by Dr. J. W. B. Douglas   v

Introduction   xi

1   The Problem Stated   1

2   Models of Attainment   12

3   A Socio-spatial Model of Educational Attainment   31

4   Measures for Models   48

5   Types of Local Authority   68

6   The Sixteen-plus Cohort   111

7   The Seventeen-plus Cohort   130

8   The Nineteen-plus Cohort   144

9   Class, Provision and Educational Attainment   153

10   Conclusion: Social Policy, Ideology and Educational Attainment   167

Appendices   175

Notes   191

Index   201

INTRODUCTION

This book reports the findings of the first half of a research project funded by the Social Science Research Council of the United Kingdom. The aim of the project as set out in the grant submission was:

> To examine the patterns of variation in the educational attainment of children from different social class and regional backgrounds. By focussing upon Local Education Authorities it is intended to discover the extent to which variations in policy and resources determine variation in educational attainment.

The project began officially in January 1972 but some very preliminary work had been carried out before that date by the two principal authors of this book. This early work developed out of a teaching programme in the sociology of education in the Department of Sociology and Social Administration of the University of Durham. In attempting to combine some of the preoccupations of social administration and sociology into one coherent course it became clear to us that a useful focal point would be the nature of Local Education Authority (LEA) involvement in the field of education. At this point in time we were quite encouraged by some of the research material available to us, particularly the work of N. Boaden,[1] G. Taylor and N. Ayres,[2] and J. Eggleston,[3] and the reports of the Northern Economic Planning Council on education services in the northern region.[4] What these reports had shown was the degree of variation in the quality of educational provision among local authorities in England and Wales, and we became aware of the urgent need to examine the implications of such variation in greater detail.

For a whole variety of quite fortuitous reasons our efforts were concentrated at this point in time on the Northern Economic Planning Region. It was an area of the country which we knew very well and for which detailed information was readily available. Also, the University of Durham has for a long time encouraged research into the north-east of England. The results of our research efforts prior to the grant application to the Social Science Research Council were published as a departmental working paper,[5] and as a paper in the journal *Sociology*.[6] The key suggestion in the *Sociology* article was that:

> the provision of educational resources by Local Education Authorities, in so far as such provision is related to the wealth of each Authority and the kinds of social policies pursued by each Authority in the Education field, is not only a neglected area of study but, more importantly, may be of equal signifi- cance in explaining variations in patterns of educational attainment than the better-documented factors associated with social class, school and family structure.[7]

We made it clear at the end of the article that further local studies were required to document in full the operation of local authorities in the field of education. In the departmental working paper, 'The Myth of the Restricted Code',[8] we tried to suggest that when the influence of variation in resources and patterns of provision by local authorities is taken into account, the explana- tory power of the variable, social class, in predicting educational attainment rates is reduced considerably. We argued that, as a result of this, it was necessary to reformulate explanations of success and failure in school. The reason we gave then was that: 'Too much emphasis on the socio-cultural factors which are taken to influence educational attainment can divert attention from the educational system itself, its institutionalised policies and the structure of its operation.'[9] Running through this paper was a criticism of recent social policy in education and the implication that much of what passes as sociological explanation of educa- tional attainment has an ideological function in obscuring the underlying mechanisms which perpetuate inequality.

We were sufficiently encouraged by the results of this work and the way in which it was received among our colleagues to attempt an extension of the project into a national study. This book, while employing slightly different methods from the earlier research, reports the results of that extended research. The overall project is not, however, complete. There are two further steps to be taken. From the very beginning we felt it was important to examine a particular local authority in some detail;

to scrutinise as far as possible the decision-making processes reflected in the national data set. This study is now in progress and is aimed at assessing the politics of a local opportunity structure. We are trying to assess the influences which determine the kinds of resources available for education in a given locality and the kinds of policies which govern the way in which resources will be allocated.

The next step in the project is to examine the way in which children at school make decisions to leave school or stay on for further study. In the end it is these aggregated decisions which are compiled into our data on attainment rates. This part of the project is also well under way. It is designed to uncover how the structure of educational provision in a given locality affects the way in which schoolchildren perceive their educational life chances and make decisions about their careers. We plan to report the results of the local authority case study and the school leaver study in a separate volume.

The present volume sets out the theoretical framework in terms of which the research reported here has been conducted together with our research findings. The first three chapters of the book deal with sociological theories of educational attainment and set out our theoretical model of a socio-spatial system. Chapters 4 onwards up to chapter 8 describe our research methods and report the results. The data we have collected describe the educational attainment rates of three cohorts who remained at school until the ages of sixteen, seventeen and nineteen years respectively in 1970. We have collected data about the kinds of schools they attended, the areas in which they lived and the level of resources which have been expended on each cohort, in order to assess what factors explain most of the variation in attainment rates. Chapter 8 looks in greater detail at the pattern of uptake of higher education awards of the nineteen-year-old age cohort and examines what it is which explains the differences among English and Welsh LEAs in this area. The results of this research and what we see as its main implications, both for sociological theories of educational attainment and educational policy, are discussed in the last two chapters.

ACKNOWLEDGEMENTS

WE should like to take this opportunity of thanking the many people who have helped us with this book, and those organisations whose resources we have had to use, and without which this study could not have been finished. The Social Science Research Council made available the funds for this study and have been very helpful in all our contacts with them. We are very grateful to the SSRC for its support. The Department of Education and Science (DES) kindly made available to us data which are not usually obtainable in a publishable form. These data added substantially to our data set, and we were very pleased to be able to have access to them.

Many people helped us with this book and are, at the time of writing, probably unaware of just how important that help has been to us. We should like to thank in particular the education officials who gave us their time in Blackpool, Rochdale, Wigan, Merthyr Tydfil, Bristol and Solihull. We are grateful to them for their very frank discussions and readiness to help us. We are also indebted to the staff of several libraries for the patient way in which they helped us to pick our way through the data sources we have used. The staff of Durham Public Library, Newcastle Central Library, Durham University Library, Newcastle University Library and the Durham Institute of Education Library all deserve our thanks.

We also wish to record our gratitude to the staff of Durham University Computer Unit for the efficient service they have given us, and in particular to Mick Youngman and Eric Tannenbaum, Computing Advisers to the Social Sciences, for their extremely valuable help and advice with data analysis. We should also like to thank Betty Gittus of Newcastle University for her helpful advice on statistical methods.

There are many other colleagues and friends whose comments on our work have been very valuable to us. The Thursday Evening Seminar of the Durham University Department of Sociology and Social Administration has been a useful forum in which to discuss some of our ideas. We extend our thanks, therefore, to our immediate colleagues and postgraduate students in the Department.

We wish to express our very great debt to Jen Syer, the part-time secretary to the research project (shortly to become undergraduate sociologist). Without her abilities as a critic and an organiser and, of course, though these have been the least important, her typing skills, the work which has gone into making this book would not have been either so pleasant or so efficiently organised as it has been.

Martin Lowe of the Medical Research Council Research Unit at the London School of Economics examined our manuscript, and particularly the data sections, with a fine toothcomb. His comments have been invaluable to us.

It hardly needs to be added, however, that the full responsibility for the way in which the book is written and for what it says is ours alone.

May 1974   D.S.B.
                                                               W.W.
                                                               B.G.F.

1

THE PROBLEM STATED

*The hereditary curse upon English education is its
organisation upon lines of social class.*[1]

So argued R. H. Tawney in 1931, and while it may be disputed
that the system is cursed, few could argue seriously that education
in Britain is not organised on lines of social class. The division
of the school system into a private and public sector, which was
the prime target of Tawney's remarks, still persists. Within the
public sector many of the elementary schools which Tawney
described as having poisoned souls and spirits blighted with social
inferiority still exist. The social outcomes of this division have
remained relatively constant over time too. The educational life
chances of middle-class and working-class children are markedly
different. Working-class children still plunge prematurely into
unpromising employment and too many schools are still so
persistently understaffed and poorly funded that their capacity
to educate is severely reduced.

Despite many attempts at reform, complex patterns of
educational inequality still persist with an intransigence which
borders on brutality, and while the idea of equality of educational
opportunity still has a mildly radical ring, few people are confident that it can be achieved. Indeed, a depressing sense of failure
hangs like a mist over the educational achievements of the last
twenty-five years. A. H. Halsey has summed it up in this way,
referring to the major thrusts of post-war educational policy as
essentially 'liberal' in conception:

The essential judgement must be that the 'liberal' policies failed
even in their own terms. For example, when, in a large number
of the richer countries during the nineteen fifties, a consider-

1

able expansion of educational facilities was envisaged, it was more or less assumed that, by making more facilities available, there would be a marked change in the social composition of student bodies and in the flow of people from the less favoured classes into the secondary schools and higher educational institutions. This has certainly not happened to the degree expected.[2]

What is more, the pre-war optimism that educational inequality would become less of a problem as real opportunities expanded has given way to a sociologically based pessimism about the constraints which severely limit a child's capacity to learn. As A. H. Halsey put it in the book from which we have already quoted:

> In summary it may be said that liberal policies failed basically on an inadequate theory of learning. They failed to notice that the major determinants of educational attainment were not schoolmasters but social situations, not curriculum but motivation, not formal access to the school, but support in the family and community.[3]

The curse, then, still remains, but we have come to think about it in a different way and adopted new measures in an attempt to remove it. Success in doing so, however, will depend upon how well we understand the connection between education and social class.

The aim of this book is to explore that connection and in so doing attempt to identify the assumptions which presently inform conventional analyses of educational inequality.

The theme of this book is that contemporary thinking about educational inequality is quite inexcusably dominated by a preoccupation with the social determinants of educability. This preoccupation is premised upon the mistaken belief that social-class differences in educational attainment reflect fundamentally different social-class capacities for learning. We shall attempt to show that differences in attainment are best explained as the outcome of a class imbalance in political and economic power, and that to argue otherwise is to confuse an aspect of the structure of society with the qualities of particular individuals.

To pursue the earlier metaphor, the curse we are concerned

with is, indeed, an hereditary one but the mechanism of its transmission is not genetic, but social and political. As such, quite unlike a genetic fault, the mechanism we are interested in is capable of change through social and political means. We are therefore not concerned with the social determinants of educability but the social structure of educational attainment.

When Tawney castigated English education for its class-ridden structure, he did so in the firm belief that it could be changed. It is clear, however, that Tawney was no utopian. He was too much of an historian to overlook the fact that elementary education and the demands of the manual labour market were related to one another. As far as he was concerned, cheap elementary education was a direct consequence of the demands of industrialists for cheap child labour and part of that demand was for a labour force fully acquainted with its position in society. To meet this demand (Tawney claimed), the schools taught working-class children to be inferior. Not directly, but through their dreary appearance, shortage of staff, shortage of books and the general assumption that, for most children, elementary education was terminal education. Were this not sufficient the working-class child finally realised his inferiority for, as Tawney put it: 'He is taught it by recurrent gusts of educational economy, with their ostentatious insistence that it is his happiness and his welfare which, when the ship is labouring, are the superfluity to be jettisoned.'[4]

In his view, schools are implicated in a wider system of inequality. A shabby society will produce its own shabby schools, not because providence ordained it that way, but because of the absence of a political will to challenge a power structure whose supporters insist on the need for a plentiful supply of cheap labour from the elementary schools. The implication is clear. In the absence of such a political challenge other reforms can have only limited effects. Elementary schools by any other name are still elementary schools.

We have here, then, two views of inequality in education, and both have profound implications for the way in which inequality can be understood and for the measures which can be taken to eradicate it. On the one hand there is the view articulated by Halsey in the quotations we have already cited. In this view inequalities in educational attainment have their roots in the social and cultural differences which divide the population into social classes. A different view, advanced by Tawney, sees social inequality as an essential product of capitalist society and of its labour market in particular. From this perspective, structured inequality is expressed not merely in the levels of education achieved by children of different social-class backgrounds but also in the quality and type of schooling children receive.

From the socio-cultural perspective, patterns of educational inequality can be expected to change given appropriate changes in socialisation techniques. Qualitative and quantitative changes towards better schooling are a *sine qua non* of this approach and have, in fact, been the principal aim of radical social reform, but even to insist on such institutional change is not to deny or underrate the crucial importance of motivational change. Without motivational changes, institutional reforms in schooling will, on this account of inequality, have only minimal effect.

For those identifying with Tawney's vision of the world, changes in the pattern of inequality in education can only come about by fundamental changes in the structure of society. Tawney's own political pragmatism led him to look with some confidence to the equalising effects of policies to rid society of the public schools and to extend and strengthen state education. But it is in the logic of Tawney's own argument that such changes can only go so far before they fall foul of an hierarchically organised labour market.

It is one of the claims of this book that these two approaches, highlighted here for the purposes of exposition, contain the essential dilemmas of post-war educational policy. It is in terms of these different positions that post-war social policy debates about educational reform have, in part at least, been conducted. It is certainly the case that the supposed failure of a reform strategy based on policies of extending and widening the base of educational opportunity, lies at the root of contemporary attempts to re-evaluate some of the central premises of the way in which educational inequality is explained.

In the British case, this re-evaluation has resulted in a mild case of pessimism, but some hope at least does remain that policies of positive discrimination in education will result in measurable payoffs in achievement. Such was the conclusion of Halsey's research.[5] In the United States, however, despair of achieving equalitarian goals through educational reform has reached pathological proportions. In an extremely influential book, which, as we shall subsequently argue, needs to be criticised for its theoretical structure and research design, Christopher Jencks has argued that differences in the level and quality of schooling and in cognitive skills are not so closely related to subsequent inequalities in life chances as had been previously presupposed. Jencks has set out his case this way:

> Those who see schools as instruments of social reform usually share a series of assumptions that go roughly as follows:
> 1. Social and economic differences between blacks and whites and between rich and poor derive in good part from differences in their cognitive skills.
> 2. Cognitive skills can be measured with at least moderate precision by standardised tests of 'intelligence', 'verbal ability', 'reading comprehension', 'mathematical skills', and so forth.
> 3. Differences in people's performance on cognitive tests can be partly explained by differences in the amount and quality of schooling they get.
> 4. Equalizing educational opportunity would therefore be an important step toward equalizing blacks and whites, rich and poor, and people in general.
> Our research has convinced us that this line of reasoning is wrong.[6]

This book by Jencks sustains some upsetting general conclusions which have shocked the educational world. Not only do Jencks' researchers claim that:

> None of the evidence we have reviewed suggests that school reform can be expected to bring about significant social changes outside the schools. More specifically, the evidence suggests that equalizing educational opportunity would do very little to make adults more equal.[7]

They also go on to argue even more strongly that inequalities in adulthood can not be affected, as it is often thought, by programmes of positive discrimination or educational compensation. They have this to say on the notion of compensatory education:

The schools, of course, could move beyond equal opportunity, establishing a system of compensatory opportunity in which the best schooling was reserved for those who were disadvantaged in other respects. The evidence suggests, however, that educational compensation is usually of marginal value to the recipients. Neither the overall level of educational resources nor any specific, easily identifiable school policy has much effect on the test scores or educational attainment of students who start out at a disadvantage. Thus even if we reorganized the schools so that their primary concern was for the students who most needed help, there is no reason to suppose that adults would end up appreciably more equal as a result.[8]

The position adopted by Jencks *et al.* is not one of resignation or the acceptance of inequality. Quite the contrary; there is a strong egalitarian thrust to the book, and a very sincere concern with what they regard as unjustifiable income inequality. The point they make is the simple one that a multi-targeted and carefully phased attack on inequality is required, and to assume that educational reform will achieve equality is utopianism carried to an absurd and unjustifiable degree. The position taken in this book is that Jencks is almost right, but for entirely the wrong reasons. Put simply, the Jencks argument that the family background of children explains 55 per cent of the variation in educational attainment needs to be very carefully qualified. Secondly, and in relation to the first point, Jencks has consistently underestimated the effects of education on adult inequality because he has equated inequality with income inequality. We shall argue that income inequalities are only a partial and very inadequate measure of inequality. Finally, Jencks' data are about individuals and not broader groupings of individuals. As J. W. B. Douglas has argued, the data analysis carried out on this basis tends to underestimate the socially more significant differences between groups of people.[9] Within broad groups such as non-manual and manual workers there will, of course, be wide differences in income. An architect and a school teacher will have different incomes yet comparable levels of education. But if we include such variables as job security, promotion prospects, fringe benefits and superannuation schemes into our notion of 'income' then the differences between non-manual workers are not as significant as the differences between non-manual and manual workers.

The problem we have to deal with, then, is that of inequality in educational opportunity at a time when conventional accounts of that phenomenon are being severely questioned. The criticisms we have briefly levelled at Jencks apply, to more or less the same degree, to the research carried out for the Plowden Report.[10] If our reaction to such work can be distilled into a simple proposition, it is that both Jencks and Plowden fail to appreciate what is involved in the notion of social class. Both reports treat the concept of social class as if it referred to specific kinds of *behaviour*; neither report uses social-class concepts to refer to particular kinds of *relationship* in society. The difference is a crucial one. If class concepts are used to describe and explain behaviour then it is logical for us to expect research into educational attainment to be designed to discover the social and psychological variables which predict educational success. This, in fact, is what most post-war research into education has set out to do. If, on the other hand, class is viewed as a relational concept, greater effort will be made to understand the structure of educational opportunity itself, and to discover the consequences for one group in society of the determined efforts of another group to achieve its own goals. Seen from this point of view, differential rates of educational attainment among different social groups are the product of competition for scarce resources and sometimes the product of conflict.

This is not the place to pursue this particular debate. It is sufficient for the moment to note that this book is offered as a contribution to this ongoing *theoretical* debate about the relationship between social class and educational attainment.

The starting point for the research upon which this book is based was a recognition of persisting patterns of educational inequality. In contemporary Britain these patterns are indeed complex. Educational life chances vary not only according to social-class background but also by place of residence. The two dimensions, social class background and place of residence, are not, of course, independent of one another, but it is worthwhile to keep them at least conceptually distinct. The reason for this is the very important one that, while social class predicts educational attainment levels with a high degree of accuracy, it is not always the case that children similarly placed in the social hierarchy perform similarly well in the field of education.

Educational attainment levels for children of the same social and economic backgrounds vary according to the region of the country in which they live. As G. Taylor and N. Ayres have convincingly shown, the division between north and south in England and Wales is still a socially significant one.[11] Regional differences conceal much more subtle and important differences. Educational attainment rates vary according to LEAs. Working-class children from Caernarvonshire have a much better chance of staying on at school and of succeeding at school than working-class children from Wigan in Lancashire. Several pieces of research have highlighted the importance of the role of local authorities playing a crucial part in the process of educational attainment itself and therefore of being a determining factor in the real structure of educational opportunity.[12]

In addition, there are variations in the structure of opportunity and in levels of educational attainment even within particular local authorities. This has been recognised for a long time. The Newsom Report[13] pointed to the poor performance of children in slum areas, and the Plowden Report[14] served to advertise a little more widely than had previously been the case the well-known fact that within British cities there were areas of acute social deprivation and educational disadvantage which required positive efforts of social intervention. These were, of course, the educational priority areas.

There is, too, substantial evidence that the school is *not* a uniform learning environment affecting all children to the same degree. Several studies of streaming and 'tracking' practices have shown this assumption to be untrue.[15]

Educational inequality is thus a complex phenomenon requiring analysis at many different levels. Part of the burden of the research reported here has been to show that the most parsimonious account of it is still one which focusses directly on the notion of social class. The variation in educational attainment rates we have referred to and which we seek to explain in this book is simply a further manifestation of the way in which the structural force of class affects life chances. In this respect, the approach to the problem of inequality developed in this book deviates from the approaches of Halsey and Jencks in two crucial respects.

Firstly, in contrast to the position Halsey takes up in his book *Educational Priority*, we shall attempt to show that liberal education policies failed, not because of an inadequate theory of learning, but because of an inadequate conception of social class. Secondly, in contrast to Jencks, we shall maintain that it is far more important to concentrate upon variations in educational attainment than upon variations in cognitive skills. We are not in the least surprised that measures of ability do not predict with any great degree of accuracy the income levels of adults. Apart from the statistical evidence, there is a much more fundamental point which needs emphasising, which we have referred to as the spatial patterning of educational life chances.

Place of residence may be a much more important variable in predicting the kind of educational career people are likely to pursue and, therefore, the kinds of occupational status people are likely to achieve, than measures of educational ability. Indeed, the National Children's Bureau study, *From Birth to Seven*, noted that on reading and arithmetic tests children from Wales perform less well than children from almost any other region of the British Isles.[16] Yet, as we shall show, children from Wales generally have higher educational attainment rates, measured in terms of their propensity to stay on at school beyond the minimum statutory leaving age. Great restraint is needed not to read too much into this observation. The National Children's Bureau researchers argued that social-class factors do not have a uniform effect on learning capacities, so that there is no direct correspondence between social-class background and measured ability. However, there is certainly a general tendency for the two to be related. The differences they detected among regions of the British Isles could be explained, they said, by different teaching practices. Whatever the explanation, we have here an indication that it is important to keep measures of educational ability and measures of educational attainment analytically distinct. Children from the English home counties may not be able to read very well by the age of seven, but they find their way into universities at a much higher rate than would have been expected, were measured ability the factor that guaranteed that kind of educational success.

We are committed to the view that there are factors other than ability which predict differences in educational life chances, and that these factors are likely to be obscured by the theoretical stance taken by some sociologists of education. We have set out in the next chapter some of the principal elements of the perspectives we intend to criticise and we make the point quite explicitly that theories about educational abilities and attainment might very well be implicated in the persistence of educational inequality. Burton R. Clarke's argument about the 'cooling out' functions of higher education is relevant here:

> A major problem of democratic society is inconsistency between encouragement to achieve and the realities of limited opportunity. Democracy asks individuals to act as if social mobility were universally possible; status is to be won by individual effort, and rewards are to accrue to those who try. But democratic societies also need selective training institutions, and hierarchical work organisations permit increasingly fewer persons to succeed at ascending levels. Situations of opportunity are also situations of denial and failure. Thus democratic societies need not only to motivate achievement but also to mollify those denied it in order to sustain motivation in the face of disappointment and to deflect resentment. In the modern mass democracy, with its large-scale organisation, elaborated ideologies of equal access and participation, and minimal commitment to social origin as basis for status, the task becomes critical.[17]

This passage reflects the basic tensions which we have referred to earlier. There is an upper limit on the possibilities of high levels of educational attainment for all children with ability. It must be comforting for those who do not succeed to be told that their failure is the outcome of their own deficiencies, and that they have lost out on an otherwise scrupulously fair educational race. It must be comforting, too, to teachers and head teachers that the failure rates of the schools they run have little to do with the way they perform their tasks. It must also be comforting to local politicians to realise that spending on schools is likely to have little effect in changing attainment rates when such rates are a product of social processes far beyond the control of the local authority. As long as everyone continues to subscribe to the notion of equal opportunities in education then inequalities in the output of different schools will remain politically unproblematic. It can only be conjecture that sociological theories of educational attainment of the sort mentioned earlier have been implicated in the process of mollifying failure that Clarke refers to. But the *prima facie* evidence that this is indeed the case is considerable. It is to this extent that we would contend that sociological theories of educational attainment are part of the problem of inequality itself.

The context of the research reported in this book is thus one in which there is considerable doubt about what kinds of strategies are required to achieve some change towards equality in educational opportunity. What this book offers, hopefully, is a fresh way of examining inequality in education and a desperately needed new data base upon which new ideas can be tested. Central to this approach is a theoretical model of a socio-spatial system. The problem we have set ourselves, then, is to explain the persistence and variation of educational inequality in modern British society.

2

MODELS OF ATTAINMENT

IN the last chapter we sketched out briefly the theoretical scaffold in terms of which the data we have collected about local authorities in England and Wales will be interpreted. Central to this structure is the notion of a socio-spatial system which defines the variables which, at this point, can only be said to relate to the observed distribution of educational life chances in this society. The precise theoretical meaning of the notion of a socio-spatial system, and the way in which it can be operationalised to generate explanatory theory, are the main preoccupations of this book. The aim of the next chapter is to demonstrate the way in which this theory can be applied.

In the meantime we feel it is important to set out, in their strongest possible form, other types of explanation of inequality in education so that the force of the explanations we shall subsequently present can be assessed. We feel it is important to do this since some of the more conventional ways of interpreting the observed inequalities in the distribution of educational life chances differ substantially from the one presented in this book. Since they are conventional, we contend that they can be seen as part of the problem of inequality itself.

At its simplest, the problem is one of knowing why educational inequality occurs in this society and from this knowledge coming to some view of what kind of social policy would modify the patterns of inequality detected. If the explanations of inequality are incorrect, then it is likely, though by no means inevitable, that the social-policy responses based upon such explanations will fail to achieve the goals they set out to achieve. This is a simple way of setting the problem. It is not seriously suggested that social policies in education, for example to set up educational priority areas or to initiate programmes of comprehensive reform, are decisions based upon the rational evaluation of educational research combined with a determined political will to realise the implications of research in social policy. Educational policy is always compromised in the real world by considerations of political support and the availability of financial resources. What is more, it is not always clear from research what kinds of social policies ought to be pursued.

Nonetheless, sociological research in education has had a profound, and not yet carefully assessed, role to play in structuring the way in which educational questions are selected and answers to those questions formulated. A quite dramatic illustration of this relationship can be seen in the way in which the whole notion of 'compensatory education' has been discussed. In an effort to overcome the 'deprivation' of 'disadvantaged' children both in Britain and the United States programmes of compensatory education, directed specifically to pre-school children, have been developed, both by the State and by private organisations. Using such instruments as the nursery school, the pre-school playgroup, the Parent-Teacher Association (PTA) and language development programmes, efforts are being made to 'enrich' the environment of deprived children.

As Morton and Watson[1] make clear, one of the central assumptions of this approach is that interventionist efforts at the early stages of a child's educational career are likely to result in positive educational payoffs at a later stage so that the otherwise cumulative effects of a disadvantaged situation can be neutralised and greater success in the wider society can, to some extent, be assured. This latter suggestion raises two questions which have not been examined as fully as one might expect.

The first question refers to the extent to which the life chances of an individual in such diverse fields as employment, housing and education are related to the educational skills he possesses. Is it true, for instance, that upward social mobility through the occupational system, with all the contingent and subsequent benefits of income security and good living conditions, depends upon the level of education a person possesses? Or, to put it differently, can it be predicted with confidence that ascending levels of educational attainment, or, at least, an ascending capacity to achieve in educational terms, is necessarily related to ascending levels of occupational achievement? If the answers to the questions were unambiguously positive, which they are not, would we then have to assume that levels of educational performance and subsequent educational attainment are themselves related to the abilities which a person possesses?

One of the themes of this book will be that there are social, economic and political factors, which, independently of the level of ability of a particular social group, operate to depress or enhance occupational and educational life chances, so that efforts to 'enrich' the environment of some children, while legitimate and desirable in themselves, cannot be thought of as improving educational life chances. Whatever else such enrichment programmes may achieve, there is as yet very little evidence that they make any significant contribution to the goals of educational equality. We shall return to this argument later, presenting a more forceful empirical evaluation of it. The point for the moment is simply that the notion of compensatory education is premissed on an assumption that ability and achievement always go hand in hand.

Furthermore, a highly significant part of this assumption is that the capacity to achieve through education is a quality which individuals possess, and that an understanding of this capacity involves an assessment of the social factors which, through the socialisation process, influence the growth of ability. Morton and Watson have described this way of assessing educational inequality as an outcome of a 'liberal ideology'. As they put it:

> It is our contention that the ideology of compensatory education is a specific expression of the liberal ideology. From this standpoint the formulation of social problems in psychological terms such as 'maladjustment', 'linguistic or sensory deprivation' and 'poor motivation' can be seen as the scientific counterpart of the individualistic approach to social problems which characterises the liberal perspective. The technical terminology of psychology thus reflects the liberal's conviction that problems are rooted in individuals rather than in the overall social order.[2]

The structure of assumptions which we have been discussing and which serve effectively to locate, as C. Wright Mills would have it, public issues – in this case educational inequality – in

terms of private troubles, is not, of course, unique to the study
of education. A similar approach, as Mills has shown, is adopted
in the United States for a whole range of questions from rural
depopulation to urban poverty. The professional ideology of
social pathologists is not, however, our main concern.

The second important question which such an approach to
education raises is the extent to which reform of the opportunity
structure of a society can be engineered through educational
reform. Or, to put the issue a little more mildly, the question is
one of deciding how far equality of opportunity in the important
markets of society can be improved by what level and kind of
educational change. We can consider later the additional complexity of how far such strategies of educational change, however
desirable, given the political end of equality, are themselves likely
to be accepted. A sociologist would need to be unusually
optimistic to believe that a policy of full comprehensivisation, for
instance, is ever likely to be put into practice, given the political
texture of many English local authorities.

It is the structure of interpretation and analysis of equality in
education which must concern us at this point, for it is in terms
of this structure that educational questions are formulated. The
example of compensatory education is only a minor example of
the issues which should concern us. The debates about education
in Britain, since the Second World War particularly, have had a
much wider focus on the structural aspects of inequality, and the
kinds of explanations which sociological researchers have thrown
up have received a sensitive hearing in the Government. Speaking
to Maurice Kogan, Lord Boyle said: 'The work of these people
made one realise that the pool of potential ability was deeper
than we'd thought, and that the interplay between nature and
nurture was more subtle than used to be accepted.'[3] And in a
conversation between Maurice Kogan and Anthony Crosland, the
former Labour Minister of Education reinforced the impression,
speaking of the way in which he involved writers like A. H.
Halsey and John Vaizey in his decision making at the DES. He
invited them around to his own house to discuss matters:

I would say that I want tonight to discuss the binary system or
university accountability or the age of transfer. The agenda
was always concerned with matters where a decision was

required. There was no general chatter – and they got no drinks until the serious discussion was over. People become much too talkative if you give them something to drink.[4]

In a much more direct way, the writings of sociologists, and the kinds of assumptions their writings have helped people to reach, have informed in a crucial way several major post-war reports on education in Britain. The Plowden Report made frequent reference to the work of J. W. B. Douglas, and also drew on the work of Basil Bernstein, A. H. Halsey, B. Jackson, J. B. Mays and D. F. Swift, among others. The Robbins Report and the Newsom Report, although mainly concerned with how to utilise previously untapped pools of ability, were influenced by current sociological and psychological theories. The following quotations are from the Robbins Report and the Newsom Report respectively:

the transmission of a common culture and common standards of citizenship . . . we believe that it is a proper function of higher education, as of education in schools, to provide in partnership with the family that background of culture and social habit upon which a healthy society depends. This function, important at all times, is perhaps especially important in an age that has set for itself the ideal of equality of opportunity.[5]

Intellectual talent is not a fixed quantity with which we have to work but a variable that can be modified by social policy and educational approaches . . . There is very little doubt that among our children there are reserves of ability which can be tapped, if the country wills the means.[6]

It is difficult to assess what impact this has had. Clearly, sociological writings have come to the notice of more people directly concerned with education. They have become part of the curriculum for the training of teachers and might, to that extent, help teachers to 'understand' the educational problems which confront them in schools. A. H. Halsey's recent book *Educational Priority*, which is a closely argued assessment and defence of policies for educational priority areas, reveals the possibility of the direct influence of research upon social policy. Liverpool Education Committee adopted one of Halsey's proposals to establish an education visiting service comparable to the health visiting services, and appointed such an officer. Further examples of the way in which research ideas have been realised could be given. What concerns us, however, is the kind of understanding of education which the literature, particularly on inequality, conveys to those who read it, and what kind of theoretical explanations of inequality this literature sustains.

THE CLASS-CULTURE PARADIGM

We have already, if rather tangentially, implied that explanations of failure to attain in the school system are marked by a set of liberal, individualistic assumptions: that the problem of failure in school is, therefore, seen more as a private trouble and not a public issue. This claim needs to be vindicated, for at first sight it does not appear to be correct.

To begin with, explanations of educational inequality have to be understood historically. For a recognition that educational life chances are not equally distributed among different members of the community is not a new phenomenon. Nor is the view that inequality, and particularly educational inequality, has no rational justification, a new one. Nonetheless, it was not until 1944 that Butler's Educational Act made an attempt in this country to make an inroad into a pattern of educational provision which had for so long favoured the richer sections of society. This Act, as is well-known, set out to achieve equality of educational opportunity and the parity of prestige between different sectors of the secondary educational system. It set out, amongst other things, to eradicate finally the pernicious distinction between secondary and elementary education which had persisted since the late nineteenth century. It was, in short, a package deal to reward the public for its war participation, to meet Labour movement demands for some concessions to equality of opportunity, to tidy up the administrative framework of education and to create a basis for future educational planning.

Acts of Parliament do not, however, by themselves, change the world. In many ways the 1944 Education Act failed. By embracing the dubious psychology of the Spens Report and thereby legitimating the creation of secondary modern schools by local authorities, the Act merely replicated the elementary and secondary system which operated before the war. By leaving detailed planning of the secondary school system to individual local authorities, the Act left the gate wide open for a series of plans and patterns of provision, with an inbuilt administrative obstacle to easy transfer between secondary schools. In particular, by insisting on selective procedures for children aged eleven, the Act virtually guaranteed, although this was not publicly admitted, that access to grammar schools was to be a middle-class right and a working-class privilege.

It is in many ways too easy to castigate the 1944 Education Act, particularly so since we now have the benefit of nearly thirty years of educational research behind us – a body of research not available to war-time planners. At the same time, however, it is essential to look critically at the 1944 Act and subsequent legislation, in order to see clearly why the Act failed. If we raise these doubts we are in a better position to assess critically the structure of assumptions which informed the 1944 Act and which now, through educational research, informs current educational policy. The point we are making is quite straightforward. If legislation is based on inadequate sociological or psychological theories either about learning potential or the interrelationship between systems of education and social structures, it is inevitable that the manifest goals of such legislation will not be realised.

In the case of the 1944 Act, one of the many reasons why it failed was the nature of the psychological theories of learning which it presupposed. The major finding of the Spens Report, that ability was a by-product of intelligence, was built into the 1944 Act and was the culmination of nearly fifty years of psychological research. Translating this research into the field of educational planning is not an easy task. The difficulty is that educational planning is about realisable social values and it is in terms of such values that research findings will be selected and interpreted. There is a sense in which intelligence is irrelevant to education, but in a society which values some notion of individual excellence it is inevitable that such excellence will be seen to depend on qualities possessed by individuals themselves. This is an example of the way in which individualism, as an old political and ethical theory, has penetrated educational thinking about human abilities. Once there was a general consensus about the validity of the intelligence=ability equation: all that was needed was a measure of each variable, and the final seal of approval was given. Intelligence tests were the instruments of that approval.

The high level message was by 1944 quite clear and unambiguous. If children do well at school it is because they have the ability to do so, and this ability can be measured. The main task of research during the 1950s and 1960s, however, was to undermine the credibility of such a psychological model of ability, and in particular of educational attainment. Several difficulties were noted in the assumptions of the Spens and Norwood Reports. One was the extent to which ability was influenced by environmental factors. What had become clear, particularly by the time the 1954 Report on early school leaving had been published, was that selective secondary school places were more likely to be given to children from families which were better off. This raised the question of just how far God had favoured the middle classes when he gave out intelligence, or whether, to be more realistic, there were factors in the home environment or social position of children which enhanced or depressed ability. It was the work of such writers as A. H. Halsey, Jean Floud, J. W. B. Douglas, Basil Bernstein, Hilda Himmelweit and many others, which throughout the 1960s exposed, among other things, the inadequacy of a strictly psychological or genetic explanation of the distribution of ability and attainment in British schools. This was particularly true of the writings of J. W. B. Douglas. In the book *The Home and The School* he produced evidence from a longitudinal study of a cohort of children born in 1946, showing that social-class factors were systematically modifying test-score performance for the children in his survey. His work in this is very well-known, but what makes it interesting for us is the way in which it highlights some kind of dynamic interaction between the child and his environment. For once such a connection is shown to exist, it is difficult if not impossible to hang on to outmoded beliefs about attainment in school being the reward for individual abilities. A major plank of the individualist position is therefore removed.

Arguments of this kind, which in short emphasise that human abilities are to a considerable extent determined by social environments, fed directly into the educational debates of the late 1950s. Anthony Crosland picked them up in his book *The Future of Socialism*, claiming that a socialist educational policy cannot be content with a weak concept of equality of opportunity. Rather, it required a strong concept in which the social, cultural and familial factors shown to be involved in school attainment could be reflected in educational planning. This, of course, was a mild plea for policies of positive discrimination in education.

What was emerging, then, was a new way of looking at the bundle of educational abilities. What was lacking, however, was a clear theoretical statement about how differences in ability emerge in the course of socialisation and of the consequences of different socialisation patterns on other aspects of the child's capacity to perform well at school. It is in this relatively un-charted territory that some of the work of Basil Bernstein immediately took on a tremendous significance. He pointed out that the child's perception of the world and the categories in terms of which that perception is organised, particularly linguistic categories, is socially structured. What Bernstein offers is a rather complex, and often misrepresented, statement about the relation-ship between social structures, especially family social structures, socialisation patterns, modes of conceptualising the world, particularly social relationships and the structure of language codes. His writings cannot under any circumstances be reduced to the simple proposition that working-class kids cannot speak properly. Unfortunately, many of his ideas have been assimilated into educational folklore precisely in this way. Nevertheless, Bernstein's work has been received, however correctly, as a kind of antidote to genetic or psychological accounts of educational performance and has been particularly important in fostering such pedagogical ideas as language development and the need for relevant curricula. A message can be read into Bernstein's work that the school and what it offers contribute as much to the process of failure of working-class children as the family and cultural background of the child. If the school transmits a culture, and uses a system of language for doing so, which is quite distinct from the culture and language patterns of working-class children, then it is hardly surprising that these children will fail. To pre-empt such failure there would have to be new kinds of curricula and/or language development programmes to change the structure of working-class modes of conceptualisation. The fact that, logically, this would have to entail, given the structure of Bernstein's analysis, a rather savage totalitarian transformation of working-class child-rearing patterns is often overlooked. Instead educationalists have focussed on the pedagogical possibilities of changing language codes.

The way in which the work of Basil Bernstein has been assimilated into educational wisdom would in itself be a tremendous topic for sociological study. For us, however, the most important point to notice is the way in which his writings, taken alongside those of others like J. W. B. Douglas, have served to shift the perspective from which educational attainment can be viewed. Whereas the thinking of the 1944 Education Act and of social and psychological research for the best part of fifty years had been dominated by an aggressively individualistic conception, the paradigm of the early 1960s was one which took seriously the effects on learning of such factors as language, family environment and social attitudes.

Basil Bernstein's work became well-known during what we would now regard as an unfortunate time. The 1960s was a time when the intellectual winds of the Atlantic were blowing strong. President Johnson's Education Act of 1965 released a good deal of Federal resources for a series of educational experiments to help transform the lot of the American poor, and in particular the black American poor. Experiments like Project Headstart attracted considerable attention on both sides of the Atlantic, and served effectively to open up further the whole question of the environmental determinants of learning.

In the United States the debate about economic opportunity and educational opportunity was taking place at this time in the context of a concern with the notion of 'cultural deprivation'. Frank Riessman's book *The Culturally Deprived Child*[7] was published in 1962, and the notion of cultural deprivation was to sustain liberal democrats throughout the 1960s both as an explanation of the stress factors in American society and as a possible lever point for social amelioration. As Norman Friedman has put it:

What seems to have happened was that the idea of culturally deprived children was successful as a trigger for legislative action because it possessed an extensive and flexible image appeal to a broad spectrum of persons and publics of various ideological persuasions.[8]

He goes on to suggest that the notion of cultural deprivation provides the Kennedy/Johnson Liberal with a plausible explanation of the educational failure of the poor. For the right winger the notion provides a convenient and perhaps a cheap way of making poor black kids respectable through programmes of compensatory education.

Friedman's claim cannot be established as a definitive one, but it is significant that the notion of compensatory education flourished in the United States at a time when burning buildings and ghetto riots provided daily headlines in American newspapers. It was, in fact, the threatening nature of urban crisis which forced on American educationists the task of rethinking their educational strategies for the inner cities, and two notions in particular tell the story of that change – cultural deprivation and the culture of poverty.

The notion of cultural deprivation contains the explanations of why poor kids often fail at school and, just as in Britain, the major variable in this failure was thought of, and still is thought of, as language. The notion of the culture of poverty added another important ingredient to the explanatory scheme. It had been argued, particularly in the United States, that the poor and those who did less well at school than they might otherwise have been expected to, lacked the appropriate levels of motivation. The work of McClelland[9] on achievement motivation and of other writers such as Kahl[10] had suggested the importance of this motivational variable. The report *The Negro Family* by Daniel Moynihan[11] finally gave such views credibility by suggesting that the poverty and failure of the American negro is to a large extent explained by the structure of the negro family itself. High divorce rates, illegitimacy, the absence of father figures, poor housing standards and a pathological failure to live for anything but the present, all combined to produce the inevitable effects of social breakdown and failure.

Very quickly, then, in the United States a view emerged in which educational failure is interpreted as a function of cognitive and motivational deficiencies, which themselves are a product of a distinctive cultural subsystem, the culture of poverty. It is worth noting too that a great deal of American research has been focussed on studies of language acquisition following directly the lead given in Britain by Basil Bernstein. This notion explains educational failure as the inevitable outcome of the cognitive and motivational characteristics of particular children, revealing again the tendency of much educational research to individualise failure. This is a somewhat idealised and simplified account of the trend in educational thinking, and the development of these concepts was certainly not so systematic, nor were they unchallenged. Another contribution to the conventional wisdom of educational research was the emerging view, on both sides of the Atlantic, that schools themselves were implicated in the educational failure of poor children.

One of the possible dangers of explaining educational failure as the outcome of individual attributes, whether psychological or cultural, is that the institutional settings in which learning takes place, particularly schools, remain relatively immune from critical scrutiny. This is even more true of whole school systems, and it was to this danger that Basil Bernstein directed the cryptic remark that: 'I do not understand how we can talk about offering compensatory education to children, who in the first place, have as yet not been offered an adequate educational environment.'[12] He went on a little later to argue that: 'The concept "compensatory education" serves to direct attention away from the internal organisation and educational context of the school, and focus our attention upon the families and children.'[13] The danger in this, as Bernstein recognises, is that, once labels like 'culturally deprived' are attached to a child, they are likely to stick, and as he puts it 'do their own sad work'.

This *cri de coeur* from Basil Bernstein was written sometime in 1969, and in many ways is much more applicable to Britain than the United States. The failures of Project Headstart and other enrichment programmes had, by the end of the 1960s, produced a critical examination of the public school system in the United States and what it had to offer. The work of Fantini and Weinstein,[14] Holt,[15] Reimer[16] and Kohl[17] had opened up a furious debate about the relevance of curriculum and the whole purpose of schooling in American society. In Britain, educational discussion was centred on the implications and relevance of the Plowden Report. British academics were thus clearly listening to the ongoing debate with a very selective ear, for the Plowden Report can be seen as the product of a particular theory – the theory of cultural deprivation – which had by this time come under severe attack in the United States. The Plowden Committee were quite explicit in stating that many of the social and educational problems of some inner city schools stem directly from inadequate resources. The famous comment in the Report that: 'What these deprived areas need most are perfectly normal, good primary schools alive with experience from which children of all kinds can benefit,'[18] illustrates the point very well. But the focus of the Report on the psychology of poverty and the assumptions which it makes about the ingredients of success in education confirm that the Report was the product of a particular way of thinking.

The research survey commissioned by the Plowden Committee and carried out by the late Professor Wiseman purported to show that of all the variables which can be associated with either good or poor performance at school, the quality of the family environment, particularly the attitudes of the family to education, was by far the most significant. Howard Glennerster welcomed this research as taking us 'beyond the unhelpful categories of social class'.[19]

From a survey of over three thousand children in 173 schools throughout the country, the Plowden Committee came to the following conclusions:

The specific contributions made by the variation in parental attitudes are greater than those made by variation in home circumstances, while the latter in turn are greater than those made by the variations between schools and teachers.[20]

What this meant was that the variable, parental attitudes, appeared to have more explanatory power in relation to the test scores of the sample children than the variable, social class background. In many ways the 'finding' is the most significant, and underlies Glennerster's response to the Report which we have quoted above. The research and the Report together seemed to locate explanations of poor educational performance firmly behind the living room door, and in the attitudes of parents. Such observations, as many have pointed out, are the direct product of a particular set of theoretical assumptions and the policy recommendations which flow from them; the idea of setting up educational priority areas and the concept of positive discrimination in particular, are themselves an outgrowth of these assumptions.

Briefly, the Plowden Committee assumed that any explanation of educational performance must apply to the development of abilities and skills in children. For this reason the Report was criticised by Bernstein and Davies for its excessively biological and psychological preoccupation with ability.[21] Secondly, it assumed that a concept like social class can only have meaning when translated into attitudes and social behaviours of particular groups of people. As A. H. Halsey has pointed out, this way of thinking about the concept of social class fails totally to recognise that social-class concepts refer to broad socio-economic divisions in society which have historical roots and structural 'force'.[22] The upshot is that social-class concepts are trivialised so that poor people and certainly those who do not do well at school are explained away in terms of what are taken to be their own social characteristics. Finally, the Plowden research is premissed on a whole set of methodological assumptions about factor analysis and regression analysis which are, despite their apparent rigour, very questionable. We will discuss research methodology more fully in Chapter 4, but suffice it to say the Plowden researchers only got out of the methodological pot what they put into it. If it is assumed *a priori*, which it was, that parental attitudes are important, and if data were collected about such attitudes, then they are clearly going to appear to be significant in any subsequent statistical analysis. At the same time the significance of this one variable is very likely to outweigh the significance of variables not included in the data set. It might have been possible to throw out a completely different set of results if different measures of home circumstances, school quality and especially social class had been included in the data set. The point here is very simple. Lying behind the empirical rigour of the Plowden research are a whole set of assumptions about the social determinants of educability and the factors which predict educational success for schoolchildren. In summary form we might list these assumptions as a set of propositions:

1. Children differ in their capacity to benefit from education.
2. The capacity of a child to benefit from education depends

upon the interaction of its psychological attributes and its environment.

3. The basic psychological attribute of the child is its intelligence measured by its intelligence quotient.

4. The important characteristic of the environment is the amount and quality of stimulation it provides the child, particularly in relation to the child's developing attitudes, motivation and cognitive skills.

5. Families differ in their ability to stimulate because they differ in their attitudes to education. Differences on this dimension are much greater than the social-class differences between families.

6. Schools are very important in fostering ability, but less so than families.

7. Positive discrimination in favour of deprived areas coupled with programmes to involve and educate parents is likely to produce significant social and educational change.

The Plowden emphasis on the quality of the home environment should not blind us to the fact that Plowden was well aware that there are few grounds for complacency about British schools.

Whereas in the United States schools were, by the late 1960s, being criticised for a wide variety of their characteristics, school criticism in Britain had been much more sharply focussed. Throughout the 1960s great concern was shown with the pernicious effects of streaming in schools and the whole process of labelling in education. The writings of Simon,[23] Ford,[24] Jackson,[25] Barker-Lunn[26] and David Hargreaves[27], amongst others, had served to question some of the pedagogical assumptions of streaming practices and to point to the way in which such practices often discriminated against working-class children. Such writers were sensitive, too, to the disparities of resource allocation among schools of different types and even within schools themselves. The Plowden Committee actually confirmed this critical account of British schools.

What had emerged, then, in the course of the 1950s and 1960s, was a way of understanding the problems of educational attainment which can be described as a class-culture paradigm. Elsewhere we have set out the basic ingredients of this approach in the form of a diagram,[28] and it is reproduced here as fig. 2.1. This diagram is a representation of the kinds of variables and

Figure 2.1
THE CLASS-CULTURE PARADIGM

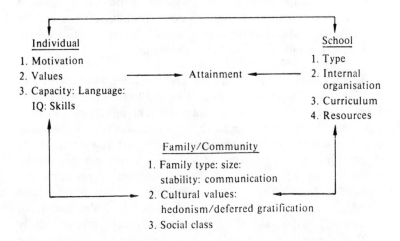

some of their suggested relationships which have been employed by sociologists in the course of their research. It asserts simply that educational attainment is a social process influenced by many factors in the home, the school and the environment of the children which bear directly on their cognitive capacity and motivational drive.

It is in terms of such a framework that patterns of educational inequality are explained. Set out in this way, however, there is a tendency to overestimate the extent to which there is consensus on every point of this approach. Such a way of looking at educational processes has not gone unchallenged. Bernstein's work has been subjected to extensive criticisms by Lawton[29] and Harold Rosen.[30] The whole literature on intelligence and ability exists in a storm of conflicting argument. Coates and Silburn, among others, have pointed out, for instance, that:

> The social structure that generates poverty generates its own shabby education system to serve it; and while it is useful to attack the symptom, the disease itself will continually find new manifestations if it is not understood and remedied. The solution to poverty involves, of course, the redistribution of income, but more than that, it requires the redistribution of

effective social power. Self-confidence, no less than material welfare, is a crucial lack of the poor, and both can only be won by effective joint action. More contentiously, it seems to us that educational provision alone cannot solve even the problem of educational poverty, if only because in this sphere there are *no* purely educational problems.[31]

The policy implications of this research tradition have themselves not gone unchallenged. Notions like cultural deprivation have been severely attacked from many different directions. At their mildest such criticisms suggest little more than the view that poor children are not really deprived at all; they are just different. At their strongest, and the work of Valentine stands out here as the most bitingly appropriate, studies of cultural deprivation are castigated for failing to recognise how society affects poor people.[32] Poverty and educational poverty, Valentine feels, particularly in the wake of the Moynihan Report, serve effectively to blame poverty on the poor.[33] The relevance of comprehensive reform as an agent of egalitarian change has been questioned from several quarters[34] and the relevance of policies of positive discrimination in poor urban areas has itself been seriously challenged.[35] In short, the debate still rages whether or not patterns of inequality in educational attainment are an artefact of the structure of capitalist society or the outcome of the not-so-private pathologies of particular groups of people. As a consequence there is considerable disagreement about the type and level of policy response, if any at all, which would be necessary to modify the way in which the system at present functions.

These disputes, it must be emphasised, are not over the amount or the quality of research evidence. They reflect instead some deep theoretical disagreements about the way in which educational processes can be explained and at one level they reflect rather basic philosophical and political disagreements about what education ought to effect in a given society.

To unravel all the points of disagreement would take a book in itself and take us too far away from our theme. The question cannot be avoided, however, since conventional ways of understanding educational attainment are clearly inadequate.

Our main point is that many of the writers we have referred to in this chapter fail to appreciate the structural nature of the concept of class. As a result they fail to distinguish between those variables relating to educational attainment which describe individuals and those which relate to the properties of the system in which people find themselves. Put another way, no firm distinction has been made between *system inputs* and *personal inputs* into the process of educational attainment.

The effect of this, as we have shown, is necessarily to personalise educational failure and to avoid the question of just how far success and failure at school are a matter of the level and quality of educational capital invested in particular groups of people. Schools and local authorities have been criticised, but, certainly in Britain, no systematic attempt has been made to measure the precise contribution which system inputs make to variations in rates of educational attainment which have been described at the beginning of this book. Both major political parties have been agreed since 1945, certainly, that expenditure on education is both desirable and necessary and for most local authorities the education service eats up by far the largest amount of their rate revenue. But what is the precise contribution of the educational system itself to educational attainment? Do the differences in resources and the wealth of local authorities and differences in the kinds of schools they provide and the policies they pursue, contribute to differences in educational attainment of the children in the schools? Who, in any case, benefits most from the education service not simply in terms of subsequent achievement but also in terms of current provision?

Answers to these kinds of questions are not so unequivocally uniform and predictable as the answers which are given about particular types of children, nor have such questions been considered to be quite so problematic. If on the other hand we face up to the two questions we raised at the beginning of this chapter, then we are forced to enquire about the structure and funding of the system itself. The questions were, firstly, how far do measurable educational skills predict attainment and future income, and secondly, how far can reform in society be engineered through reform in education?

There is no simple answer to the second question, but it does at least raise questions about the relationships between education and society. The question about education and income has been analysed time and time again, but never in such a way that researchers have been prompted to examine system inputs in relation to attainment. The debates of the 1960s in Britain about educational inequality were nearly all premissed on the perfectly valid assumption that ability was being wasted. What we need to find out about now is whether this wastage is in any way systematic. Are wastage rates to be seen as the aggregate of thousands of misinformed, disinterested decisions about the worth of education, or the predictable outcome of the structure and operation of education systems at national and local levels?

In several earlier publications we have attempted to give some kind of answer to that question. We have argued that system inputs and differences in those inputs do, in fact, explain a great deal of the variation in attainment rates among local authorities in England and Wales. What is more, we attempted to set out a different theoretical perspective from which to ask such questions. The results of this work confirmed for us, at least, that there was something systematic about failure and success, but to understand it required new theoretical models and a renewed research vigour. The aim of the next chapter is to describe the framework of such a theoretical perspective.

3

A SOCIO-SPATIAL MODEL
OF EDUCATIONAL
ATTAINMENT

In the last chapter an attempt was made to show that some of the main accounts of educational inequality, both in Britain and the United States, derive their theoretical strength from a particular view of the nature of social stratification. While it would be unfair to make too strong an accusation that writers in this area have failed to understand that relationships between social classes are relationships of competition, sometimes conflict, and certainly relationships of power, it is nonetheless true that structural examinations of class have not been systematically carried out.

We are not suggesting here that sociologists of education are ostriches: that they fail to see the world of unequal opportunities, for this is palpably untrue. In a recent paper castigating among other things the levels of economic inequality in this society, the inadequacies of the liberal vision of a future, fairer society, and the way in which the concept of social class itself has become trivialised, A. H. Halsey has written:

> A theory which explains educational achievement as the out-
> come of a set of individual attributes has lost the meaning of
> those structural forces which we know as class. An adequate
> theory must also attend to those structural inequalities of
> resource allocation which are integral to a class society.[1]

Having argued that: 'Theories postulate paths to stated ends, therefore to test the validity of a theory is to evaluate the

effectiveness of a policy which expresses it,'[2] Halsey concludes
with the comment that an adequate theory of educational
inequality, i.e., one which recognises the structural forces of
class, would result in clearly radical social and political policies:
'The translation of such a theory into action would require
political leadership with the will to go beyond the confines of
traditional assumptions.'[3] He does not state explicitly what such
policies would be. However, he does make clear that the assumption of steady progress towards a fairer society is as false as it is
diversionary, and that to explain inequality as the outcome of
private troubles is clearly inadequate. However, A. H. Halsey
concludes with a plea, and does not indicate what kind of analysis
would be involved if we were to take seriously the notion that
class is a structural force.

The aim of this chapter is to set out the theoretical basis for
the kind of study we feel is required. As we cannot condense into
one chapter an account of the structure and operation of modern
urban social systems, or give an adequate account of the kind of
research upon which our notion of the socio-spatial system is
based, our main aim is to identify the key components of this
perspective.

Three basic working propositions are central to the notion of
a socio-spatial system. Firstly, the concept of social class, as we
use it, refers to a relationship between groups differently placed
in society to realise the main rewards of society. The various
parameters of inequality are seen, from this perspective, as the
outcome of different social and economic placings. Some groups
in society are simply more favourably placed to purchase and
gain control of those facilities and institutions which are essential
in the drive to improve market situations. To this extent the
concept of class is identical to that of Max Weber.[4] Secondly,
the relationships between social-class groups are relationships of
control and domination. The instrument of such domination is
power, which is a complex phenomenon. It can include the direct
application of violence, or the skilful manipulation of symbols,
concepts and ideas. In short, ideologies sustain the power to
control the behaviour of other people or to legitimate existing
social relationships. When such legitimation is successful,
economically dominant groups can retain a monopoly of goods,
services and income. Despite the existence of inequalities that

dominance is not challenged. In such circumstances power becomes authority and those with authority come to have special rights and duties.

Applied to education and the unequal distribution of educational life chances, this perspective leads to the suggestion that such inequalities persist over time, to some extent, precisely because they are legitimated. Tawney grasped the essence of this argument when he pointed out that secondary education for working-class children was 'rationed like bread in a famine', while middle-class children receive such education as of right. The paradox of this situation is that glaring inequalities can persist without being fundamentally challenged.

The third component of this perspective is that the rewards which accrue to different social groups in society are spatially distributed. We attach considerable significance to this last element of our analysis. In simple terms a spatial system only describes the distribution of a commodity or resource throughout a given population. From this elementary perspective it is known that educational resources vary considerably among different regions of the country and local authority areas. The same is true of the whole range of social services. Such variations are described clearly by G. Taylor and N. Ayres.[5] The spatial distribution of social services has been carefully documented by Bleddyn Davies.[6] Housing life chances are spatially distributed in city areas. Cities sustain housing areas differentiated according to the social-class position of various groups. This was noted as long ago as 1844 by Friedrich Engels[7] and has been a continuous theme in studies of poverty since the turn of the nineteenth century.

Such observations can, however, take on a quite different meaning. They can be seen, and, we would argue, must be seen, as reflecting the distribution of real income in a society.

It is extremely important that we do not have a restricted conception of income. The notion of real income includes much more than current after-tax income. It refers to the value to the individual of such things as social service provision, housing amenities, transport facilities, access to open space, the quality of education available in a given locality, the provision of medical services, employment security, fringe benefits and pension rights.

In addition, the value of real incomes has to be seen in a time perspective. Changes in the value of private property produce changes in real income. The economic mechanisms involved are complex, but connections exist between property booms and inner city dereliction; investment decisions and unemployment; interest rates and school building programmes; inflation and the real value of teachers' salaries. Such changes and decisions will have a subsequent impact on the market situation of different social groups. The question then becomes 'Who benefits?' which in turn questions the nature of the principles of territorial justice which operate in this society.

Pahl has suggested, on this question of territorial justice, that the operative principle is not one of need.

> If the provision of public services followed such a principle systematically, we would expect to find a positive correlation between the need for public services and facilities and their provision. Thus, the Welfare State and notions of citizenship would be a reality and the inequalities following from wage differentials would be compensated for, so that the poor would not be doubly penalised. However, it is a commonplace to observe that this does not happen, although the detailed documentation presents many complicated methodological problems.[8]

If we apply Pahl's comment to education facilities, its relevance becomes even more apparent. The Newsom Report made clear in 1959 that schools with inadequate buildings and resources were concentrated in areas of cities which were disadvantaged along other axes.[9] A similar distribution of educational resources prompted, in the case of primary schools, the recommendations from the Plowden Committee that a programme of positive discrimination in educational planning was required to offset the increasing problems of urban poverty.[10]

These comments were specifically directed at educational facilities. We shall demonstrate presently that education facilities are a component of real income and that such facilities are of strategic importance to the individual, as a key factor in his future real income. For the moment it is sufficient to note that social-service provision, of which education is a major component, is not made according to the principle of need. What we tend to find are concentrations of, on the one hand, high levels of real income, and, on the other, low levels of real income, which have become increasingly polarised. The suburb and the slum symbolise both extremes. Nor can we explain these distributions as the outcome of random historical processes, although there is a clear historical dimension to their distribution. To say that spatial variation is a result of historical processes is simply a way of restating the problem. It is essential that theory and research go beyond such responses and unravel the mechanisms involved in historical processes.

We contend that these spatial distributions are the outcome of differences in the effective social powers different groups in society can command, to secure advantages for themselves. We would also maintain that, in any study of variations in housing provision or education opportunities, it is important to examine the relationship between the social groups in question, in an historical context. The physical fabric of cities, the patterns of residence and the quality of social-service provision all reflect, in the last analysis, the relative power and claims of different social groups on the real income of the community. The resolution of such claims, we argue, is what ultimately determines the social structure of opportunity.

SOCIO-SPATIAL SYSTEMS

The notion of a socio-spatial system directs attention to the social, economic and political processes which influence the structure of opportunity and the distribution of real incomes in society. The most recent formulations of the concept of a spatial system are to be found in the writings of R. Pahl, and take as their starting point the way in which real incomes are distributed in an ecological context.

In the case of Pahl the main thrust of socio-spatial analysis is to discover the 'hidden mechanisms' of distribution in urban economies, to create a greater understanding of territorial justice and social stratification. As he puts it:

> The hidden mechanisms of redistribution operate in socialist as well as in capitalist societies: one of the tasks of a radical

sociology might be to expose such mechanisms and to consider how an understanding of the urban redistributive system can be used to develop new theories of stratification in industrial society.[11]

The theoretical complexity involved in dealing with such a problem is enormous. Pahl would agree with David Harvey that a clearer understanding of spatial process is not likely to be achieved if urban analysts stay too close to the myopic confines of single disciplines. The city, as one kind of spatial form, is a complex structure requiring interdisciplinary analysis. As Harvey states:

> Any general theory of the city must somehow relate the social processes in the city to the spatial form which the city assumes. In disciplinary terms this amounts to integrating two important research and educational traditions – I shall call it building a bridge between those possessed of the sociological imagination and those imbued with a spatial consciousness or a geographical imagination.[12]

The difficulty, which Harvey recognises, is that few people have such a spatial consciousness, and that little research employing socio-spatial concepts has been conducted. *Born and Bred Unequal* by G. Taylor and N. Ayres[13] is described by the authors as a study in social ecology. It could, therefore, be treated as an example of socio-spatial research. However, the study lacks a theoretical backbone, and offers no more than painstakingly accurate statistical descriptions of income distribution. Perhaps one exception to this criticism in sociology is the paper by John Rex on 'the zone of transition' in the urban area.[14] Building upon Burgess' notion of the ecological structure of the city, Rex incorporates into his theoretical model of the urban housing market the notion that groups are differentially placed to realise housing life chances, making it possible to identify distinct 'housing classes'. These housing classes, e.g., private owners, council tenants, and those who seek rented accommodation – and in this last category Rex is particularly concerned with coloured immigrants – can come into conflict with one another. The conflict, he maintains, is likely to be mediated through the political system of the city, so that the final balance of advantage and reward in the housing market is an outcome of differences in the political power of different housing classes. As Rex himself puts it:

> In the class struggle over housing, qualifications either for a mortgage or a council tenancy are crucial. They are, of course, awarded on the basis of different criteria. In the first case size and security of income are vital. In the second 'housing need', length of residence and degree of affiliation to politically powerful groups are the crucial criteria. But neither mortgages nor council tenancies are available to all so that either position is a privileged one as compared with that of the disqualified. It is likely, moreover, that those who have council houses or may get them soon will seek to defend the system of allocation which secures their privileges against all categories of potential competitors. Thus local politics usually involves a conflict between two kinds of vested interest and between those who have these interests and outsiders.[15]

One important implication of this view is that forms of discrimination, and in particular racial discrimination, are not explained as the outcome of deep-seated attitudes of prejudice. Such attitudes may well exist, but they explain neither the response of the host population to immigrant groups nor the associational response of immigrants themselves. The relationships between host and immigrant communities are being forged at the anvil of the housing market and cannot be explained adequately in any other terms.

Housing, as a form of income, can thus be seen as an outcome of the market power of different groups in society. Housing is a particularly crucial commodity since it constitutes the basis for future gains, or losses, in income. A change in the value of property in an upward direction clearly increases the wealth of the owner-occupier. If, on the other hand, a motorway box were to be built in the immediate area of the property in question, its value may go down, although the real income of the community may go up.

Such an effect is known technically as an external or third party effect. Through a preoccupation with 'externalities', some planners and urban economists have reached outward for some concept of a socio-spatial system to uncover the process by which some groups in society are more favourably affected by planning decisions than others. We can thus detect some convergence between sociological conflict models of the urban system and economic theories of 'externalities'.

Pahl has suggested that we need to recognise that systems of income distribution and resource distribution in urban contexts are controlled by 'gatekeepers', and that conflict is endemic in the urban system. He explains it in the following way, and we quote from his paper extensively:

(a) There are fundamental *spatial* constraints on access to scarce urban resources and facilities. Such constraints are generally expressed in time/cost distance.

(b) There are fundamental *social* constraints on access to scarce urban facilities. These reflect the distribution of power in society and are illustrated by

bureaucratic rules and procedures;

social gatekeepers who help to distribute and control urban resources.

(c) Populations in different localities differ in their access and opportunities to gain the scarce resources and facilities, holding their economic position or their position in the occupational structure constant. The situation which is structured out of (a) and (b) may be called a socio-spatial or socio-ecological system. Populations limited in this access to scarce urban resources and facilities would be the dependent variable, those controlling access, the managers of the system, would be the *independent* variable.

(d) Conflict in the urban system is inevitable. The more the resource or facility is valued by the *total* population in a given locality, or the higher the value and the scarcer the supply in relation to demand, the greater the conflict.[16]

EDUCATION AND INCOME

In introducing the notion of the socio-spatial system we have stressed that we are dealing with a system of real income distribution and we have referred to the field of housing as an example. There is no theoretical reason why this notion should not be extended further to encompass any other facility valued by the community. Education is yet another important example. Pahl himself has used the example of education to develop his notion of the socio-spatial system further. He has written:

> By way of example let us consider the non-random distribution of a facility, which differs in its quality even though it is distributed to all the population within a given age-range; education provision is known to vary considerably between L.E.A.s. Variation in expenditure by L.E.A.s can be shown by comparing annual expenditures per pupil on books and stationery: this gives some measure of the importance education holds in the overall budgetary planning. It is of course extremely difficult to get good quantitative indicators of such things as the quality of education, but size of class, turnover of teaching staff, age of buildings and so on might be combined to provide an index of educational quality for a given school area. Hence for those *at the same position in the occupational structure*, different localities will offer different degrees of educational opportunity.[17]

The crucial sentence is the last one. For it can be demonstrated that inequalities in access to educational opportunities generate, in the longer term, inequalities in income opportunities. The calculations are extremely difficult, but if the return to the individual of investment in education is seen as a form of investment in human capital, there are real differences which can be identified between educated and uneducated groups in society. The work of M. Blaug,[18] E. F. Dennison[19] and R. K. Kelsall[20] suggests that investment in education, as a form of investment in personal human capital, pays off. Ascending levels of education are paralleled by increases in personal income, and the differences between educated people and non-educated people over a lifetime of earnings are very substantial.

There has been considerable debate recently over the precise nature of variations in educational level and variations in incomes among groups. Christopher Jencks has suggested that educational levels do not predict income levels, even for those with identical educational careers.[21] Great care needs to be exercised in evaluating this argument. It may well hold in the case of individuals, but it is far more important to carry out such calculations for groups. J. W. B. Douglas made precisely this point in a critical review of Jencks' work,[22] but the point needs further reinforcement. Evidence for such a comparison is rather scant, but it is clear that no comparison is valid which deals with such an atrophied concept of income which Jencks employs. This type of analysis fails to recognise that differences between manual and non-manual income levels, even on a net earnings criterion, are far greater and more socially significant than income variations within these two groups.

One immediate difference which must be taken into account in such a comparison is the realistic expectation of many non-manual workers for rising incremental incomes, job security, high benefit pension rights, fringe benefits and an increasing and firmly based capacity to raise credit for mortgages, cars and other kinds of expenditure. Even if we were to leave outside our calculation the incremental increases in a person's market position, which derive from changes in the real value of a person's property, it becomes clear that simple comparisons of net earnings lead to a totally false impression of the distribution of real incomes in a community. As Goldthorpe and Lockwood pointed out a long time ago, there is far more to the notion of market situation than current earnings.[23]

The *prima facie* evidence is, then, that the market position of manual and non-manual groups in society is remarkably different. The evidence for current income differences is unambiguously clear. The work of B. Abel-Smith and P. Townsend,[24] A. Westoby and G. Williams,[25] J. Meade[26] and A. B. Atkinson[27] speaks almost with one voice. Income distribution in this society is skewed in favour of the better-off. On the question of job security and promotion aspects, Dorothy Wedderburn[28] has pointed to further differences between manual and non-manual groups in this society.

Evidence of the sort we have referred to needs to be seen in another context, in which standards for occupational selection are being gradually raised for a host of occupations not previously restricted by special entrance criteria. Many non-manual occupations have been operating selective entry standards for a period. The obvious examples are those of medicine, law and the other professions. The Crowther Report noted that the increasing rate of technological change and occupational specialisation was creating demands for further educational certification: 'there is a growing tendency for many occupations, which do not absolutely require a specific expertise for their performance, nevertheless to demand an attested standard of general education for entrance.'[29] The Crowther Report, correctly we feel, interpreted this trend as an outcome of an excess in the supply of labour from the age group of the immediate post-war period, referred to usually as 'the bulge'. Historically, however, this has not been the impetus behind restricting occupational entrance in non-manual occupations, and particularly elite non-manual occupations.

The generalisation can be made, with some historical force, that entrance requirements into the older professions and the civil service have stemmed from deliberately planned attempts to retain a status monopoly for upper-middle-class occupations. In this sense, the establishment of formal entrance requirements can be seen as an occupational strategy to bolster the effective market power of different occupational groups, by operating on the supply of potential recruits. The economic logic is simple. If the supply of a particular kind of labour power can be restricted, the price it can command on the open market for labour will be increased, and the claims for such benefits as job security, pension rights and fringe benefits will correspondingly increase.

These consequences may not underly the expressed reasons for occupational selectivity, but the effects of selectivity are still the same. Therefore, if we employ a much wider concept of income, it becomes clear that education and income are inextricably bound up with one another. Educational life chances, for those people who rely on the sale of their labour power for income, determine income life chances. The existence of private schools, of course, indicates the way in which this relationship works in its pure form. If educational life chances can be purchased, as they clearly can be, then a system of income inequality is being, as it were, doubly reinforced.

An examination of the income consequences of public schools is not our most crucial task. What we must do is give some account of how the system of income distribution works in practice and is influenced by the extent and distribution of power in society.

POWER AND SOCIO-SPATIAL SYSTEMS

Class, we have argued, is a structural force in society, and we cannot gain an understanding of the concept if we neglect the fact that class positions differ in the amount of power which can be commanded by groups differentially placed in society. Class, too, is a multi-dimensional concept. The very mention of the word, for most sociologists, triggers off thought sequences of a thoroughly confused kind, in which the accumulated conceptual junk of post-Weberian research is rearranged to describe a world of permeable status ranks, false consciousness and pluralist politics, run and controlled by ever-changing power elites.

What is required is a recognition that the structural notion of class implies relationships between groups in society who are differentially placed to realise life chances. Such groups are in a constant state of conflict, although they may not realise the conflict situation in which they are implicated. Political processes, even at a local level, can often be seen as processes of conflict, sometimes institutionalised, in which class groups are activated either to protect or to enhance their real incomes.

In this approach, urban gatekeepers, such as educational administrators and planners, are not simply rational bureaucrats: they are implicated in a political context, in such a way that their actions will influence the distribution of income, in the broadest sense, and life chances. Even the resources which gate-keepers have available – in particular resources which derive from local taxation – are either limited or enhanced by political behaviour.

Max Weber once suggested that the danger of bureaucracy was that questions of politics would be reduced to questions of administration. He was almost right. His expectation, however, is too strongly stated and leaves unanswered the question of how far politics can ever be reduced to administration. We suggest that administration is political and that the political component cannot be defined out of it. It is in this respect that our notion of the socio-spatial system begins to diverge from the view held by Pahl and other writers who have been concerned in one way or another with planning externalities or, as Norman Dennis uses the term, 'planners' blight'.[30]

We have a much more overtly political conception of educational planning and decision making than some writers would accept. This point is well illustrated by the work of Norman Dennis[31] and Jon Davies.[32] In his book, Norman Dennis was concerned with slum clearance programmes in an area of Sunderland, and Jon Davies deals with an abortive attempt to revitalise an old area in Newcastle-upon-Tyne. Both writers focus their attention on the way in which planning departments in local authorities are politically and intellectually divorced from the communities for which they plan. Both writers portray what Davies calls the 'evangelistic bureaucrat' building into his plans whole sets of assumptions which can run counter to the standards and folkways of the people for whom the plans are being made. In both books a clear picture emerges of bureaucratic insensibility, sometimes incompetence, but far more importantly, an inability of people effectively to control the planners. It is an inability which is also shared by local councillors.

Jon Davies sums his argument up this way:

> Planning, in our society, usually results in conflict, for it is in essence the attempt to inject a radical technology into a conservative and highly inegalitarian economy. The impact of planning on this society is rather like that of the educational system on that same society: it is least onerous and most advantageous to those who are already well off or powerful, and it is most onerous and least advantageous to those who are relatively powerless or relatively poor. Planning is, in its effect on the socio-economic structure, a highly regressive form of indirect taxation.[33]

Unfortunately Davies does not manage, in the end, to prove this point directly. Norman Dennis, whilst not saying so explicitly, would seem to agree with Davies. Dennis makes reference to a report made by the Sunderland Medical Officer of Health in 1936, which showed that the effect of being rehoused actually reduced the size of real incomes for the families involved. This possibility is a theme which occurs throughout his book.

Rehousing and council house building are not necessarily solutions to people's housing or income needs. Dennis is, in fact, particularly sensitive to the possibility that comprehensive schemes of redevelopment to improve an area can backfire; that they can have unintended effects on income. Both writers concentrate on the world view of the planner and the structure of the organisation in which he works. They effectively defuse the planning ideologies of their more bizarre assumptions, although planning as such is not examined as a political phenomenon which redistributes income differentially throughout a community. What is examined by both writers, and Dennis is the most systematic in this respect, is the relative powerlessness of tenant groups in the face of planning decisions. In this sense they would concede the political nature of planning.

We would claim that planning is a political process, and that its political character, clearly discernible in the housing field, is equally clear in the field of education. Whatever justifications are given for planning decisions – aesthetic, technological, strategic or expedient – such decisions always occur within a structure of assumptions about the legitimate claims which different groups in society can make on public resources. These claims are made within a system of constraints, particularly through the mechanism of rates, so that plans are inevitably curtailed to fit in with an existing system of power and control.

These constraints have a historical character. The problems which Jon Davies and Norman Dennis describe are problems of social-class relationships of an earlier period. The historical precipitates of such relationships are areas of poor housing and areas of suburban redevelopment; of concentrations of old school buildings structurally inadequate for modern concepts of educational practices, and new schools at the outer rings. The outcome of such distributions are populations differing in market position and life chances and, perhaps more importantly, differing in the extent to which they can exert control over urban gatekeepers to inject some change in the pattern of distribution of real income in the community.

In this sense the notion of the socio-spatial system is not a mechanistic one by any means. The possibility does exist that formerly disadvantaged groups can come to exercise power, to redirect the allocation of important resources in the community. The whole concept of community development rests on this possibility, as do some of the more recent attempts to redefine the nature of urban education.[34]

In chapter 5 of this book we describe the efforts of some local authorities to modify the social structure of opportunity, with varying degrees of commitment and success. There are, however, limits on the extent to which the mechanisms of distribution in spatial systems can be modified.

Structures of educational opportunity have to be seen as compromises, as we have outlined in the perspective above. Certainly there is no sense in which such structures are ordained by providence. The history of educational provision in modern British society is punctuated at every stage with bitter political disagreement. The ideological and legal disputes over comprehensive reform are just the most recent chapter of such conflict. However, it would be wrong to infer that such political debate resulted in frequent innovation.

Conflict over education occurs within the political institutions of the state and the local authority. It concerns the level of funding of the educational service and the spending priorities within that service. It concerns the educational policies to be pursued and implemented. It concerns the building and siting and closing of schools, the reorganisation of schools, the drawing-up of school catchment areas, and extends over the whole day-to-day decision making of the local authority. In such circumstances the final shape of educational provision in a given area will be politically determined. It will, in short, be the product of the distribution of power in a given locality and in society as a whole.

In this respect it is to be expected that education will reflect what key groups in society regard as important educational aims and these in turn will reflect what such groups regard as important social and economic needs. Historically, of course, such needs have always been defined in labour market terms. The history of the raising of the school leaving age illustrates this point quite well. For many years British employers opposed the raising of the school leaving age because it would interrupt the continued supply of juvenile labour into the factories.[35]

It does need to be emphasised, however, that the labour market is a fundamental constraint on the education service of any society. In a given locality the labour market sets the boundaries for social-class formation. The labour market is the most important source of the real income of any community. To that extent it sets limits upon other aspects of real income such as housing provision, and through that the potential rate revenue of a local authority. Essentially it is rate revenue which determines the level of local authority wealth, and opportunities for public investment.

These, then, are some of the factors which operate on structures of educational provision and through them upon the attainment of schoolchildren. So far, we have not attempted to quantify such factors and measure their precise influence upon the overall variation in educational attainment. In the next chapter we set out a way of operationalising the notion of a socio-spatial system. The remaining task of this chapter is to underline how this way of thinking about life chances is a radical departure from the class-culture paradigm discussed in chapter 2.

From the perspective of spatial system analysis, life chances in education are deeply implicated in the logic of operation of a social market economy. What can be provided as a framework of opportunity is determined, ultimately, by the character of local labour markets. What is provided as education is the outcome of political compromise. What can ultimately be achieved by any group of children is limited by the hierarchical character of work organisations. In short, educational attainment is a public issue not a private achievement, an artefact of the distribution of power in society rather than the distribution of intelligence.

The LEA is an important and fundamental factor to be studied from this perspective. In England and Wales local authorities have the discretion, under the 1944 Education Act, to determine the character of local educational provision. They supply by far the greatest proportion of educational expenditure from their own rate revenues and they differ greatly from one another in terms of wealth, social composition and patterns of educational attainment.

The interdependence of the social, economic and political variables mentioned so far poses many methodological problems. For the purposes of this study we take the following variables as measures of the most important dimensions of the socio-spatial system.

1. Class background,
2. Local environmental factors,
3. Local authority policy,
4. Local authority resources,
5. Local authority provision.

Our intention is to relate these variables to a sixth, educational attainment. Our methodology, which will be described subsequently, involves the analysis of multivariate data, describing the elements of the socio-spatial system outlined already. We aim to disentangle which variables exert most influence on the process of educational attainment, and the pattern which such attainment follows.

4

MEASURES FOR MODELS

THE objective of this chapter is to provide a bridge between the first part of this book and the presentation and interpretation of the results of the research project, which constitutes the remainder of our discussion. The research project was established specifically to clarify the issue of the comparative importance of system inputs, as against personal inputs, in determining socially significant educational attainment.[1] The task of this chapter is to present and clarify the methodology by which we have attempted to do this.

There are two main aspects to our methodology: firstly, the analytical techniques we have used, and secondly, the assumptions about research method which underly our use of these techniques. The methods we employed consisted of a battery of multivariate analyses of data relating to three 'cohorts' of children who remained at school beyond the ages of sixteen years, seventeen years and nineteen years, respectively, in 1970. Through these techniques we have attempted to develop causal models of the process of educational attainment.

In this attempt we accept Blalock's position,[2] and particularly his claim that in the use of multivariate analyses of data sets it must be recognised that particular multivariate procedures imply 'causal models'. In other words, the use of multivariate procedures in data analysis presupposes that theoretical models or assumptions are being tested, although in some cases these models may not be explicitly stated. We feel that it is essential to make the theoretical model explicit, and use the appropriate analytical techniques to test the implications of these models.

In general then, our position is that theoretical models precede the use of analytical procedures, and that particular care must be taken to employ procedures which fit the approach suggested by 'theoretical' considerations. In this context this means that, apart from the use of cluster analysis procedures to yield a series of typologies of English and Welsh LEA's, the main analytical strategy employed will be multiple regression analysis and canonical correlation.

THE RESEARCH PROJECT

In chapters 1 and 3 of this book we have discussed the idea of an educational socio-spatial system, and described the main features of this concept. The data which we have collected for our empirical investigation are, therefore, spatially defined: that is, data which allow us to describe variables in our theoretical model as they relate to different geographical areas of the country. The use of such data attracts criticisms from two directions, both of which must be dealt with.

The first is that the use of spatially organised data conceals significant relationships. Bowles and Levin made this point in their criticism of the Coleman Report and its methodology; particularly in relation to the report's measures on school expenditure:

> The averaging of expenditures among all of the schools in a district imparts a severe bias to the data, for the available evidence indicates that the variation in expenditures among schools within a district is likely to follow a systematic pattern.[3]

We agree. However, the point that Bowles and Levin were making was that the use of ecologically defined data about attainment, at a level beyond the school, will tend to *diminish* the impact of the system upon attainment. In other words, the use of district or LEA data is conservative. We agree with this contention and we also agree that it is necessary to pursue the system down to the school, to examine the local socio-spatial system described in chapter 3. Indeed, the second part of our research project is designed to do precisely this.

What we have done is to relate the attainment of *all* children in LEA areas to provision variation in those areas. This will still mask the effect of variations within a given area, especially when variations in educational provision correspond with variations in the residence patterns of socio-economic classes, as we suspect they do. It is therefore to be expected that our results will *under-estimate* the strength of systems variables.

The second sort of criticism of this kind of research procedure is summarised by saying that it is subject to the 'ecological fallacy'. The difficulty with ecological correlations normally is that properties of individuals are related to properties of areas. In our research this is not done, in that we are relating like with like, that is, the properties of spatially defined cohorts with properties of the cohorts themselves (longitudinally ordered provision) and with general properties of the space that defines the cohorts (class background and general environmental factors). In this instance our spatial aggregates, i.e. LEAS, are, as we state in chapter 3, not arbitrary and unrelated units about which we collected data, but essential components of our theoretical model, relating to the idea of an educational socio-spatial system.

The problem with ecological correlations is that correlations among aggregate variables are higher than the corresponding correlations for individual variables. When the units of study are the aggregates themselves, then there is no problem. If we are looking at the properties of a socio-spatial system then our units are the aggregate populations defined by that system, and there is no issue. If our unit of interest is something else, then we may be dealing with cross-level inference. This would be a major problem if we were interested in individuals. We are not. The only other 'units' of interest to us apart from socio-spatial classes are socio-economic classes – another set of aggregates. Making inferences about this set in terms of another, which is what we do when we test out the model represented by Figure 4.1 by partial correlation procedures, may involve some difficulties. However, they are not the normal ones involved with ecological correlations.

J. L. Hammond, in a recent authoritative article, has commented that:

Cross level inference need not be . . . a 'game against nature'; it can instead be based on the applicability of social theory to the situation one is investigating.[4]

Given the probable existence of socio-spatial systems within LEAS, correlations for socio-spatial aggregates will be less than if we could directly determine correlations for straight socio-economic class aggregates. What interests sociologists are social classes. Individual-centred studies discount relationships of structural importance by reporting individual correlations. Sociologically speaking, this is a far greater problem than the reverse.

In chapter 3 we defined some of the components of the educational socio-spatial system represented by the LEAS in England and Wales. We can now present the elements of the educational socio-spatial system in more operational detail.

CLASS BACKGROUND

Before 1974 English and Welsh LEAS varied considerably in terms of the social-class composition of the populations resident in them. None could be described as homogeneous, some having a much higher proportion of their occupied adult male workforce in 'white-collar' or 'upper-class' occupations than others. Similarly, they varied in the educational backgrounds of their adult populations. We have operationalised the idea of class background in three ways; two of which are derived from occupational background, and one, for a more limited data set, relating to educational background.

The first is derived from data collected from the 1966 Sample Census, to yield information on the proportion of what we call occupied adult males, who are resident in the LEA area, located in the following groups:
1. High social class, i.e. professional, managerial, self-employed and intermediate white-collar workers,
2. Middle social class, i.e. supervisory manual, routine white-collar and skilled manual, and
3. Low social class, i.e. semi- and unskilled manual workers and personal service workers.

The second measure also involved use of 1966 Sample Census data to yield information of a similar kind on the proportion of non-manual and manual occupied males resident in the area.

The last measure involved the use of data from the 1961 Census on the educational background of persons aged twenty-five and over in the LEAS, for which we collected information about the proportion of males and females respectively who left school at fifteen years of age or less, for all LEAS outside Greater London.[5] This seemed to be a fairly good measure of the educational background of the parental generation of people who were sixteen, seventeen and nineteen plus in 1970 (the subjects of our three cohorts).

Thus we can operationalise the idea of class background for an LEA in terms of the composition of the occupied adult male workforce resident within it in 1966, and in terms of the educational background of persons aged twenty-five and over resident within it in 1961.

LOCAL ENVIRONMENTAL FACTORS

LEAS vary considerably in terms of environmental factors, particularly in terms of housing conditions and the degree to which the area is industrialised. In addition they vary in size, and in terms of the density of their population. All these things, which we subsume under the general heading of environmental factors, could be of some importance to the educational attainment of children. Indeed, G. Taylor and N. Ayres have claimed that the 'total material environment' of children plays a major part in depressing or enhancing their educational life chances.[6] We have used eight variables to describe environmental conditions in an area. These are:

1. Degree of industrialisation,
2. Proportion of domestic hereditaments where rateable value is below £101,
3. Comparative size of rate deficiency grant,
4. Population size,
5. Population density,
6. Proportion of households inhabited at high density,
7. Proportion of 'shared' dwellings with all basic amenities,
8. Proportion of all dwellings with all basic amenities.

Thus we have here a set of indices which together form a composite description of housing conditions, degree of industrialisation and density of population in an area. These measures will help us to identify, at one extreme the suburb, and at the other extreme the slum.

LOCAL AUTHORITY POLICY

As we have stated above, LEAS are political entities and they vary in the policies they pursue. Obviously the pattern of educational provision itself is the main consequence of policy. However we thought it would be useful to obtain some measures of 'policy' which indicated the political texture of an LEA. We have four variables which might indicate this. These are:

1. The amount of rates called in in relation to the total rateable value of LEA areas,[7]
2. The extent of Labour control of the authority,
3. The proportion of households in the area resident in council houses,
4. The proportion of children aged thirteen in comprehensive schools.

These seem to us to be an indication of the extent to which an LEA can be located to the left of the political spectrum, and, with one exception, they are not specifically educational measures.

In practice we found that while these variables emerged as important indicators of policy types in the cluster analysis, they were not correlated with attainment in the zero-order correlation matrix in any simple or straightforward fashion. It seemed to us that in fact the best indicator of 'policy' type was therefore cluster membership, and we are now proceeding to an analysis in which cluster membership is used to erect a set of dummy variables demarcating policy types. However, we are not entirely happy about the use of such dummy variables in causal modelling, and have not completed these analyses at the time of writing. In any event, it seems to us that the cluster analyses themselves sustain the account of policy role suggested. Nonetheless the absence of any proper treatment of policy is a serious weakness in the multivariate analysis, precisely because it precludes taking account of conscious working class political action in influencing levels of educational provision in different authorities.

RESOURCES AND PROVISION

It is very difficult in practice to disentangle the educational resources of an LEA from the educational provision it makes. We have employed the measure of penny rate per pupil in an LEA, which is a measure of the autonomous resources of the LEA. However, so much of educational expenditure is centrally financed that it is not a good measure of overall resources.

Provision measures, therefore, incorporate a resource element. We have used a number of measures, some of which relate to the type of school which pupils attend at thirteen years, the remainder describing pupil/teacher ratios (both primary and secondary), degree of overcrowding (again both primary and secondary), and various 'per pupil' expenditures. The remaining variable[8] describes the proportion of the teaching force who were graduates.

We consider this to be a crucial variable as it indicates what proportion of the educational system in the secondary schools of an area is genuinely 'secondary', as opposed to 'elementary'. Very generally, we can say that graduate teachers teach in secondary schools, and that they teach examination-oriented courses rather than others. Eggleston[9] has demonstrated that the provision of courses is a 'cause' of attainment.

The proportion of an LEA's teaching force who are graduates exemplifies this historical legacy and important division in education in this country, between those who take examinations, and get on to an educational and occupational escalator, and those who do not. Graduate teachers are by no means necessarily better teachers than non-graduates, but normally they provide the 'achievement' system. Earlier, proportions of children in grammar schools would have been much the same measure, but the spread of comprehensivisation and the shift in emphasis in other non-grammar schools, now masks the obvious administrative distinction.

EDUCATIONAL ATTAINMENT

What concerns us here is socially significant attainment, or evidence of having got on to the educational escalator. We feel it is therefore necessary to use three kinds of measures of attainment. The first is the proportion of pupils remaining at school beyond sixteen years, for LEAS. The second is the proportion of pupils remaining at school beyond seventeen years. The third is a set of 'rates of entry' into different forms of higher education.

There are some further, more general points to make about our data sets. All the variables employed are fully described in Appendix A of this book. This appendix gives the exact operational definition and source of each variable. We use three data sets. The first, which describes 162 of the 163 LEAS in existence in 1970, we describe as the cross-sectional data set. Essentially it contains data organised around the base year 1970.[10] The second and third are longitudinal sets. They contain data relating to the school experience of children who were sixteen-plus, seventeen-plus and nineteen-plus years of age in 1970. In other words, provision and attainment are chronologically ordered. The first of these sets contains 160 member LEAS, i.e. all LEAS but three, where boundary changes[11] had made longitudinal data of any kind impossible to obtain. However, as Outer London Boroughs are included in this set, no provision data prior to 1964 could be utilised.[12] The final data set contains 139 LEAS, i.e. all LEAS outside outer London for which chronologically ordered data describing primary and secondary provision could be obtained. Finally, it should be noted that some of our data is classified by sex, i.e. attainment and school types at thirteen years were arranged on the bases of 'Boys', 'Girls' and 'All' data. This means that some examination of differences between the sexes has been possible.

The arrangement and organisation of the data sets is of considerable importance for the analyses we conducted. The discussion of the methodology inherent in these analyses, taken together with the preceding discussion of the nature of our data, is the basis upon which we have operationalised the idea of an educational socio-spatial system, to which we now turn.

THE CROSS-SECTIONAL DATA SET AND CLUSTER ANALYSIS

We have available 69 variables describing 162 of the 163 LEAS existing in 1970, in terms of social-class composition, environmental factors, policy, educational provision and the educational attainment of relevant cohorts in that year. Some of the data we have available in the longitudinal data sets were not available for Outer London Boroughs for 1970. This was particularly the case for the proportion of the teaching force who were graduates. DES data on overcrowding in schools was also unavailable. The data on 'parental' educational experience, which came from the 1961 Census, were likewise not available for Outer London Boroughs. Some of the data in this set did not describe the situation in the LEAs in 1970 but related to the results of the 1966 Sample Census. At the time we carried out our analysis these were the most recent data available. Of our 69 variables, we decided to treat 21 variables as relatively insignificant, and did not incorporate them in the cluster analyses. These 21 were detailed descriptions of minor 'per pupil' expenditures. Thus, in the cluster analyses described in chapter 5, we used 48 variables.

The objective of this section is to clarify the nature of the cross-sectional data set, relate it to the idea of an educational socio-spatial system, and explain why we feel that cluster analysis is particularly suited to explaining that system in the context of a cross-sectional data set.

The cross-sectional data were organised around the year 1970. They represented a snapshot picture of the situation in that year, albeit that the snapshot was somewhat out of focus.[13] The elements in that picture were the components of our conception of the educational socio-spatial system, listed above. As these data were cross-sectional it was unsuitable to generate causal models. There were two reasons for this. In the first place, on a single year basis some of the data we utilise are of such a form that they cannot be used to create causal models, unless chronologically ordered. Some elements in our system have a symmetric rather than recursive relationship,[14] and recursivity is a general requirement of available methods to construct causal models.[15] However, as inspection of our general correlation matrix will show, chronologically ordered data, which are of necessity recursive, are far more highly correlated with attainment than their cross-sectional equivalents. The reason for this is that the availability of chronologically ordered and longitudinally arranged data permits the construction of a 'natural experiment.[16] These points will be expanded in relation to subsequent discussion of analyses of the 'longitudinal' data sets.

The cross-sectional data set is, however, eminently suited to another objective, which is the generation of a typology of LEAS. We have available a description of almost all LEAS in terms of a number of indices, representing the elements in our postulated socio-spatial system. It should be possible to generate from these data a typology of LEAS in terms of relationships which exist among the sets of these elements.

In general, given our account of the nature of the educational socio-spatial system, we would expect to find that there would be a concentration of LEAS where high social class would be related to good environmental conditions (a useful general description of non-educational 'social income'), high provision and high attainment. The exceptions would relate to policy, where we might expect the conscious pursuit of egalitarian educational policies to modify the general relationships. In this case, policy would be related to good provision and good attainment, but would not necessarily be related to high social class. Indeed, since egalitarian policy is a function of left-wing politics in general, it would be related to 'working-class' populations.

In fact, there is available a set of procedures which enable us to identify these groupings of LEAS and the characteristic relationships among such variables. These are the procedures collectively known as 'cluster analysis'. A large number of methods fall under this general heading, but we have used only two of them in a conbined form. These were Ward's method of hierarchical fusion, in association with the relocation method.[17] Ward's method involves comparison between individuals, on the basis of similarities between them. In practice the method calculates dissimilarities and locates the smallest. Thus with 162 local education authorities there are $\dfrac{162 \times 161}{2}$ possible combinations of two. The procedure locates which of these represents the least dissimilar pair and places them together to form a cluster. The procedure then continues forming new clusters on the basis of error, generated by fusion, until the one cluster stage, containing all cases, is reached. The process is thus one of hierarchical fusion.

Ward's method produces a series of partitions so that at each level every case is allocated to one cluster. The method ·reduces the number of clusters by one at each cycle. Significant levels can be identified by plotting the error measure associated with each fusion, and the resulting dendogram reveals levels where relatively dissimilar groups have been brought together. This indicates significant typologies composed of relatively homogeneous groups. Information about these groups in terms of the mean for group members of the input variables (plus standard deviations, F ratios and t ratios) can be obtained, and these permit descriptions of the groups.

Relocation is similar in objective to Ward's method. The major difference is that it starts with an initial grouping of the cases. The centroid of each group is computed. The dissimilarity between each case and all clusters is computed, and each cluster is placed in the group it most resembles. This process continues until the clusters are stable, i.e. there is no change of membership or relocation. Fusion in relocation involves the combination of the two most similar clusters followed by relocation of cases. Information about clusters is produced in the same form as in Ward's method.

What we have done with the cross-sectional data set is to use Ward's method to identify significant grouping levels, and then use the cluster groupings generated at that level as input into a relocation analysis. In other words, we have used Ward's method to yield a set of clusters, and relocation to ensure that cases are in the clusters which they most resemble. Ward's method alone does not do this, as once a case is located in a cluster it stays there.

One further facility of cluster analyses (both Ward's method and relocation) is that certain variables may be 'masked' from the analysis. In other words, they are not employed in computing dissimilarities, i.e. in generating the typology. Nonetheless information about generated clusters in terms of these variables can be obtained. This masking has the advantage of screening the most significant variables, and is therefore founded on theoretically based assumptions about important elements in yielding a typology.

The effect of using cluster analysis on the cross-sectional data set is that we can generate typologies of LEAs in terms of the information we have about them. The results of such analyses and discussion are the content of chapter 5 of this book. At this point we wish to outline the value and status of such typologies. One author has recently remarked:

> One of the classic debates in the history of science turns around the proper role of typologies in the development of theory. While in principle it may be apparent that the very existence of a reasoned typology ought to imply a set of interrelated propositions, and the associated conditions under which they hold – that is, a theory – not a few observers have been convinced that in practice typological construction often distracts attention from the formulation of more explicit, more powerful, and more precise propositions.[18]

Cluster analysis clearly does not produce explanatory propositions, but by generating typologies, suggests what such propositions might be.

In this context we contend that class, resources, policy, provision and attainment will be associated in particular ways. Chapter 5 will show that they are associated in ways compatible with our account.

One important issue which we have not discussed is how we treat 'non-systematic' factors which may influence educational attainment. Although this is relevant to the discussion of the analyses we conducted on the cross-sectional data set, it is better discussed in the context of causal modelling.

THE LONGITUDINALLY ORDERED DATA
SETS AND CAUSAL MODELLING

Two of the data sets we employed were not cross-sectional but were longitudinally ordered. The distinction between these two was simply that one contained all Greater London LEAs and almost all other LEAs in England and Wales and the other contained only non-London LEAs. The reason for this was that, due to London government reorganisation, some variables were not available over time for London cohorts in 1970, since the Outer London Boroughs had not existed throughout their school life. Thus one data set included more provision variables than the other.

Both were longitudinally ordered in the sense that the provision variables employed related to the actual school experience of those remaining at school until various ages in 1970. In other words, we looked at primary provision for the years during which people who were sixteen in 1970 were in primary school, rather than relating primary provision in 1970 to rates of staying on beyond sixteen years of age in 1970. This has the advantage of ensuring that the relationship between provision and attainment was reciprocal. Attainment in 1970 cannot 'cause' provision before 1970.

The effect of this is that the chronologically ordered data sets permitted the examination of what has been called a 'natural experiment'. We have measures of social-class background, environmental factors and policy in LEAS. All these were located at one point in time, normally 1966 or 1970, but, with the possible exception of policy,[19] they are all indices which are fairly stable over time. We have provision data relating to the actual primary and secondary school experience of the cohorts remaining at school until 1970. Finally, we have measures of their proportionate attainment. We thus have something like a set of measures of the operation of the educational socio-spatial system over time. The importance of this time element was discussed in chapter 3.

The way in which we used these measures and the way in which we see the educational socio-spatial system operating is presented diagrammatically in Fig. 4.1.

Figure 4.1
THE EDUCATIONAL SOCIO-SPATIAL SYSTEM

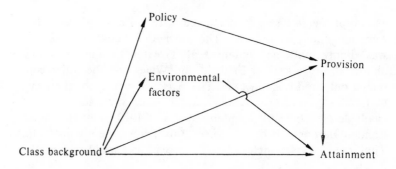

The diagram suggests that the social-class background of an LEA influences the attainment of cohorts of schoolchildren passing through its schools in the following ways:

1. Directly, i.e. in terms of 'personal', socio-cultural and familial inputs,
2. Through the relationship between social-class background and environmental factors,
3. Through the relationship between social-class background and educational provision,
4. Through the relationship between social-class background, educational policy and educational provision.

With the exception of the relationship of class with policy/provision/attainment, we would normally (in terms of our views on the nature of the educational socio-spatial system) think of high social class as being associated with good provision, good environmental conditions and high attainment. However, low social class could be associated with radical policy, high provision and good attainment.

Fig. 4.1 is a theoretical causal model. It is a representation of relationships which we suggest ought to hold. The advantage of the longitudinally ordered data sets is that they can be used in association with various multivariate procedures, to see if such relationships did hold. In other words, we test out our causal models. Kenneth Land has said that

The causal model is:

A procedure for bridging the gap between sociological theory on the one hand and the results of classical statistical analysis on the other . . . the essential idea of the causal model involves the construction of an over simplified model of reality in the sense that the model considers only a limited number of variables and relations out of the universe of social reality. Using the results of past research and current theory, the causal model is written as a set of structural equations that represent the causal processes assumed to operate among the variables under consideration. The structural equations, in turn, lead to parameter estimation procedures and evaluation of the model. The outcome of the empirical evaluation process is either the corroboration or reformulation of the causal model. Finally, the inadequacies of the model should precipitate a reconstruction of the substantive theory that generated the causal model at the outset.[20]

It should be stressed here that causal modelling based on correlations never proves causal relations. It merely demonstrates consistency. The causal ordering is a consequence of reasoning based elsewhere. Thus in a causal model the 'theoretical' assumptions underlying it must be specified. In testing our model, the following assumptions apply:

1. The non-systematic effect of social class on attainment is regarded as a residual, i.e. we order our analyses in such a way that all effect of variation common to social-class background and levels of educational provision is assigned to educational provision. This means that we assert that, in explaining educational attainment, the first thing we have to look at is the educational system itself. We see social-class composition as affecting educational attainment through its relationship with levels of educational provision.

2. After account is taken of the relationship between social-class background and levels of educational provision, we then assign the effect of all remaining common variation between social-class background and environmental factors on educational attainment to environmental factors.

3. Thus we treat the non-educational and non-environmental effects of social class as a residual.

What this means is that, on the basis of historical and general sociological perspectives in this area, we assert that 'social class' affects educational attainment primarily through its relationship with two interrelated socio-spatial systems, one distributing educational social income and the other distributing non-educational income.

We think it would be difficult to challenge the first of our assumptions. To do so would be to deny education to the educational system and locate it elsewhere. It is rather easier to assert that our measures of housing conditions and the degree of industrialisation are in reality indices of the socio-cultural background of people inhabiting particular areas, and that our approach should be rather to make class background paramount here. We disagree for two reasons.

The first is that none of our provision variables gives a good measure of physical capital in education.[21] We consider that, on the basis of the kind of evidence produced by the Newsom Commission,[22] areas of poor housing and dense industrialisation are likely to have older and less adequate schools. This does not simply relate to the physical fabric. Rather, the fact that an area is served by schools which are essentially old elementary schools, has distinct social implications. These are likely to be, in the secondary sector at least, old elementary schools retaining the 'social' perspectives of such schools, i.e. non-achievement. What Pahl says of housing is, in our view, equally true of education:

> The sheer permanence of the built environment means that the distribution of economic rewards which creates a social structure at one period of time becomes fossilised in, say, the housing situation at a later period of time when the values and structure of economic rewards in the structure has changed.[23]

Secondly, we feel that the negative effects of overcrowding, shortage of rooms for doing homework and so on, are important in themselves. In one way, therefore, our measure of environmental factors describes the domestic educational environment, not in terms of acculturation processes but in terms of simple ability to have somewhere quiet to work.

Our position on the 'residual' nature of the impact of sociocultural factors is supported by Gastil: 'In my own work, I think of culture as a residual category to which one may attribute those differences between groups that are not attributable to more general factors.'[24]

We subsume under the heading 'culture' all 'personal inputs' of groups. In the context of our study the most important of these is specifically cultural, i.e. a different familial socialisation process for working-class, as opposed to middle-class, people. This is the personal input of the group that concerns us. We reiterate here that we are looking at group differences and not differences among individuals, although the two are interrelated.

We now turn to a description of the actual methods we propose to employ in evaluating our causal models. In practice we employ multiple correlation plus a variant of partial correlation (multiple-partial correlation). In other words, we use simple regression analysis. We considered employing canonical correlation (essentially, regression analysis with more than one dependent variable) but felt that in practice this was not suited to a partition of the data set into elements causal to attainment and attainment, although it may well be a useful device when the data set is partitioned into class elements and elements describing educational provision and environment. At the time of writing we are engaged in analyses of this form. We also considered the use of path analysis, but for reasons specified in note 26 below, we felt that this method was inappropriate in testing our models.

For a description of the Blalock-Simon procedures, Van de Geer states:

> What it comes down to is that the researcher postulates a model of causal relations, draws a diagram, so to speak, where he indicates, by means of arrows from one variable to another, how causal influences might run. The model is then 'tested' by trying to derive from it which partial correlations should vanish and which should not. The derivations to be tested might be extended to higher-order partials, and could include hypotheses about multiple-regression as well. For instance, if Xa is a determiner of Xb, and Xb in turn influences Xc, whereas Xa has no direct effect on Xc, then r ac. b should vanish. Also, the multiple correlation Rc.ab should not be larger than the zero-order correlation rbc.[25]

The use of path analysis is well described by Duncan, Land and Heise.[26] A full description of the principles of path analysis is given in Land's article. For our purposes the most important element in this procedure is the meaning of the term 'path coefficient'.

> The statement that Pij is a *path coefficient* means that Pij is a number such that Pij measures the fraction of the standard deviation of the endogenous variable (with the appropriate sign) for which the designated variable is *directly* responsible in the sense of the fraction which would be found if this factor varies to the same extent as in the observed data, while all other variables (including residual variables) are constant . . . *The squared path coefficient* measures the proportion of the variance of the dependent variable for which the determining variable is directly responsible.[27]

A path coefficient is not the same as a partial correlation

coefficient. In fact, all coefficients are standardised regression weights. This has some implications which require expansion in the context of the data sets we employed and the model we wish to test. The meaning of the model suggested by Fig. 4.1 and its implications for analysis are so important that some expansion is necessary here.

The whole issue revolves around the meaning of the term 'class'. Let us for a moment scrutinise the weakest use of 'class', which refers to common situation in relation to a system allocating life chances. As an heuristic device we can think of 'educational classes', meaning spatially located groups of children in relation to educational provision. Similarly we can think of 'socio-environmental' classes. If we were to think of socio-economic class, educational class and socio-environmental class as three 'independent' groups, then we would want to assess the independent effect of all three class backgrounds upon educational attainment. Given that they are interrelated, we would be confronted by the problem of multi-collinearity and indeterminant solutions for the 'independent' effects.[28]

The implication of our assumptions 1 and 2 above is, clearly, that we do not think of these as independent. Rather, we are asserting that educational class and socio-environmental class are dimensions of a general class system based upon the dominant social and economic relationships in society. This is why we use socio-occupational categories as indices of social 'class'.

Our problem is to assess how far one of the most important spatial systems of resource allocation, i.e. education, is related to the general hierarchical structure of society, and the distribution of power within that hierarchy. Clearly education is not independent of a system of social stratification. As we have already argued in chapter 3, systems of education are inextricably bound up with systems of power and domination. This point is rather obvious when made in relation to earlier periods. Coleman has written, for instance, that: 'In nineteenth century England, the idea of *equality* of educational opportunity was hardly considered; the system was designed to provide *differentiated* educational opportunity appropriate to one's station in life.'[29] In the middle of the twentieth century the notion of equal opportunity is an important one, and although the relationship is less obvious it still persists. For this reason, it is inappropriate to distinguish between education classes and socio-economic classes. Both can be unequivocally assigned to the 'general class' relationship between socio-economic class and any other dimension of structured inequality. This means that the issue of multi-collinearity which we discussed earlier is no longer problematic. What we are concerned with is the way in which the educational system, the socio-environmental system and patterns of belief and action of different groups in society relate to one another, as three dimensions of 'class'. In this context partial correlations are particularly valuable.

THE HISTORICAL USE OF QUANTITATIVE DATA

This last point raises the question of what general status we assign to the procedures we have employed in constructing causal models. It cannot be stated too strongly that we regard these as procedures facilitating a quantitative, *historical* study. The literature on causal modelling seems to be dominated by a concern for the establishment of a positivistic and quantitatively inductive social science. It would be unfortunate if sociologists were to follow psychologists and econometricians into the models and out of reality.

What concerns us is the social context in which education is located. Quantitative investigation is a way of looking at that fundamental historical process, but it is not necessarily a better approach than any other. We employ quantitative techniques because our study demands such an approach. Thus the results we obtained are discussed and evaluated within a historical perspective about the relationship between education and social stratification. Thus our model is preoccupied with the nature of historical processes and not mathematical assumptions.

One final point to make in this chapter is that there will be no discussion of statistical significance in this book. We deal with populations, not samples from them. Some of our data is derived from the 10 per cent Sample Census of 1966, and to use the estimate yielded from that source might be a source of measurement error, but we think that for units as large as LEAs it is far outweighed by simple rounding. We deal with populations: one of which consists of almost all LEAS, one which consists of all except 2 LEAS, and one population with Greater London excluded. Inference is therefore substantive and not statistical.

In the next chapter we discuss the results of our cluster analyses.

5

TYPES
OF LOCAL AUTHORITY

As we explained in the last chapter, we subjected our data about LEAS to cluster analysis. The expectation was that through cluster procedures we could accurately identify different types of local authorities. Our theoretical expectation was that if there was any connection between the structure of educational provision, policy, level of resources, social-class composition of an area, and its rates of staying on at school, then the main cluster groupings would reflect such connections. We would expect, for instance, that local authorities which score highly in terms of resources available for education and in levels of provision will also score highly in terms of our measures of attainment.

As we shall show, this expectation is, to a large degree at least, confirmed in the cluster analysis but the result requires careful interpretation. Cluster analysis does not generate results capable of validating or invalidating theories. In this sense it is not an analytic procedure in the same way as multiple regression techniques. It is rather a way of scanning data prior to further analysis, a way of using a large body of data describing a large number of individual cases which closely resemble one another.

We employed cluster analysis to help in this data scanning process, but also in order to identify a number of local authorities for further more detailed study. In the original grant application to the Social Science Research Council we had envisaged visiting many local authorities to learn more about the data we were using in the study. We also wished to learn more about the way in which political and economic constraints in a given locality served to shape educational policy. In addition, since we suspected that the political character of the Local Education Committee might be a significant variable, underlying not only the kind of policy being pursued but the way in which resources were allocated, we felt it was important to find out more of the way in which policy is evolved and legitimated. Cluster analysis helped us in this process as we were able to identify particular local authorities as being part of a much larger but similar grouping, so that our visiting programme was considerably reduced. We have visited five local authorities representing five of the six main clusters we have identified. We also include a description of an authority representative of the sixth cluster.

The visits made for the purpose of this study all involved interviews with education officers and the interviews were, in the main, of an unstructured, exploratory nature. We have decided to report the results, however, since the cluster analyses and individual reports on each local authority together serve to highlight something of the different context in which educational attainment takes place and to indicate more clearly the strength and weaknesses of the study's data base.

In particular, we wished to explore in a little more detail the constraints which different local authorities have to face in formulating their educational policy. Local authorities clearly differ in their level of total resources, and they differ, too, in the kinds of principles they employ in the allocation of scarce resources. From the data we have collected there is no way of finding out what such principles are, or what influences them.

There are important historical differences which limit or enhance the capacity of an authority to pursue its educational policy. High expenditure levels may reflect the desperate efforts of a poor industrial authority to replace old Board Schools. On the other hand, it could reflect the political belief of a particular local elite that a high level of educational expenditure is something desirable in itself. A history of excellent educational provision may have resulted in a local authority having a good stock of excellent schools, so that current capital expenditures do not need to be high. In such a case it would be a gross mistake to imagine that low expenditure on education indicates a lack of concern on the part of the local authority. But it is precisely this kind of consideration which is obscured in the resource and provision measures employed in the subsequent data analysis.

Table 5.1

LEA CLUSTER ANALYSIS (6 CLUSTERS) (POPULATION SIZE AND DENSITY MASKED)

	Nat. av.	Cl.1	Cl.2	Cl.3	Cl.4	Cl.5	Cl.6
Rates of staying on: 16 + ...	33·0	25·7	44·9	29·9	41·5	31·2	41·3
Rates of staying on: 17 + ...	18·3	13·2	26·4	16·1	22·9	17·3	24·2
Secondary modern	44·1	56·4	48·2	5·6	4·8	62·3	30·2
Comprehensive	32·2	11·5	15·1	89·5	85·0	11·6	49·5
Grammar school 1	24·3	32·2	40·0	6·8	10·1	25·7	20·3
Grammar school 2	16·4	17·1	22·6	3·5	8·2	20·7	18·5
University awards	71·9	46·1	114·5	58·3	78·5	71·8	83·5
FE 1 awards	72·1	48·8	92·9	57·9	77·8	69·4	132·4
FE 2 awards	25·0	20·6	16·5	20·0	10·2	28·5	67·2
Teacher training awards ...	57·9	46·1	65·5	63·6	43·2	60·5	80·9
Pupil/teacher ratio: primary	27·3	27·8	26·8	27·5	31·8	27·3	21·0
Pupil/teacher ratio: secondary	17·8	18·0	17·6	17·8	17·0	18·1	16·9
Penny rate per pupil	2·7	2·4	3·8	2·3	4·6	2·6	1·8
Teachers' salaries: primary ...	66·3	66·0	65·3	63·0	66·4	64·9	89·5
Teachers' salaries: secondary	115·2	109·2	114·8	129·3	124·0	108·9	125·7
Debt charges: secondary ...	25·8	23·6	25·2	28·8	24·0	25·2	31·2
Total expenditure: primary ...	102·4	99·0	103·5	98·5	105·2	100·3	135·4
Total expenditure: secondary	188·2	190·3	192·6	187·6	206·8	180·9	204·7
Industrialisation index ...	14·5	21·6	9·9	17·5	16·4	11·7	11·8
Rate call/total rateable value	72·0	75·9	67·0	77·2	70·6	69·2	76·7
Low rateable value	83·5	92·4	55·6	92·8	60·1	87·0	95·8
Resources element: rate support grant	15·5	15·4	2·9	16·1	0·0	18·0	44·3
Population size	31·3	25·6	34·3	19·2	55·2	37·9	11·1
Population density	9·4	14·4	9·9	11·9	22·1	5·3	0·3
Labour control	35·9	70·9	9·7	57·6	46·8	20·2	18·9
High social class	14·6	9·4	23·3	12·0	15·3	14·7	16·2
Middle social class	55·3	55·8	55·4	55·4	59·0	54·7	52·4
Low social class	26·8	32·9	17·9	29·4	23·3	26·3	27·7
Non-manual	31·2	23·2	46·4	27·0	37·3	30·8	29·0
Manual	65·3	75·4	50·1	69·8	60·4	64·5	67·3
Owner-occupiers	47·9	38·1	57·9	44·2	44·4	50·4	51·8
Council tenants	25·5	32·8	16·6	29·4	19·7	25·3	18·7
Private tenants	21·8	25·0	22·1	22·7	29·6	18·9	19·9
High density	5·6	7·1	3·6	6·6	5·2	5·2	4·2
Amenities 1	25·0	18·2	26·1	19·9	17·9	28·8	41·1
Amenities 2	72·0	64·7	82·8	68·5	66·3	74·5	66·3

NOTE: The first six variables were differentiated into 'boys', 'girls' and 'total'. As there were no significant differences between the sexes, we have used the totals only, although 48 variables were included in the analysis.

Similarly, our data does not allow us to distinguish between formal educational provision and informal provision. In the case of one local authority we visited – Solihull – it is clear that the *per capita* financial input into education is grossly underestimated by the statistics of the Institute of Municipal Treasurers and Accountants. PTAS in Solihull contribute a great deal of money to the schools. In this sense the data we have about educational provision are likely to *underestimate* what is provided in a given local authority area. But it is precisely such difficulties which need to be taken into account in interpreting educational statistics. For this reason every effort must be made to gain some understanding of the social and political structure of education in a given local authority. The visits we have made represent a very inadequate attempt at gaining such an understanding. However, in the next stage of our research project we intend to conduct an intensive study of one local authority.

We now turn to a brief description of the six clusters. The descriptions we give are built up from the data set out in Table 5.1. The units of measurement for each of the variables listed are set out in Appendix A.

CLUSTER 1

The areas falling into cluster 1 are unequivocally working class, and predominantly Labour controlled. These are the towns so often described as the depressed industrial areas of Britain, the industrialisation and depression seemingly inseparable. Many northern towns, whose industrial legacy has often meant large scale unemployment, figure prominently. George Orwell's Wigan and the Lancashire landscapes depicted by L. S. Lowry provide graphic descriptions of this type of area.

The poor material environment of these areas is evidenced by high population and household densities and the poverty of social amenities in the community.

LEAS in such areas, although varying to some degree in the type and quality of their educational provision, sustain this picture of relative deprivation. The attainment rates for such areas are characteristically low, both in terms of the numbers of children remaining at school beyond the statutory minimum leaving age, and in terms of numbers entering further and higher education.

Where the level of unemployment is high, teenage unemployment or increasing mobility is likely to be a common feature of these areas.

The provision of secondary education is based upon a selective system, retaining traditional grammar schools with an extremely high proportion of pupils attending secondary modern schools. Expenditure tends to be concentrated upon secondary education with consequently low provision for primary education. However, pupil/teacher ratios for both primary and secondary schools are average.

LEAs falling into this cluster would include Barnsley, Bootle, Merthyr Tydfil, Norwich, South Shields and Wigan.

CLUSTER 2

The social-class background of areas in cluster 2 is clearly non-manual, and largely upper-middle class. Such areas are likely to have a highly mobile population. Significantly, LEAs falling into this cluster are counties, rather than county boroughs, largely concentrated in the south. These areas embrace the rich suburbs and commuter belts serving large industrial centres. They are typically Conservative controlled authorities, with a minimal degree of industrialisation. Housing is predictably largely owner-occupied, and the high rateable value of such areas reflects the high quality of social amenities.

Educational provision is governed by a selective procedure with few comprehensive places. The types of school complement the wealth of the area, with a high proportion of direct grant and independent schools.

The quality of educational provision in terms of per pupil expenditure is high, although expenditure on teachers' salaries is below the national average, which probably reflects the available supply of teachers in such areas.

Rates of attainment conform to these high standards in terms of high rates of staying on beyond sixteen and seventeen years of age. Entry to further and higher education similarly reflects high achievement, particularly entrance to university.

Such local authorities as Bath, Berkshire, Cheshire, Croydon, Solihull and Surrey fall into cluster 2.

CLUSTER 3

Areas in cluster 3 are typified by the 'average' quality of educational provision and all the characteristics of the area. They could not be described as rich or poor areas, although the preponderance of manual occupations and the patterns of housing tenure and housing density suggest a lower-middle class population. Such areas tend to be fairly industrial large towns, and are Labour controlled, although not so consistently as in cluster 1.

Educational provision is distinguished by an almost fully comprehensive secondary system. The quality of provision, in terms of expenditure per pupil and pupil/teacher ratio in secondary schools, again sustains this average picture, whereas primary school provision based upon these indices is below average.

The attainment rates for these authorities are similarly just below average in terms of staying on beyond sixteen and seventeen years of age. The pattern of uptake of further and higher education is also below average and assumes a uniform pattern throughout all sectors of further and higher education.

LEAs falling into this cluster are Cardiff, Doncaster, Gateshead, Newcastle-upon-Tyne, Rochdale and Sunderland.

CLUSTER 4

LEAs falling within this cluster are also characterised by an almost fully comprehensive secondary educational system, but differ from cluster 3 in their high attainment rates. Figures for staying on at school beyond sixteen and seventeen years are well above the national average, while awards to university and fuller value awards in further education (e.g. polytechnic courses, HND, etc.) and teacher training are also very high.

Provision in terms of expenditure per pupil is exceptionally high, especially for secondary education, and similarly expenditure on teachers' salaries for secondary education is high.

It is only in this cluster that the expenditure variables penny rate per pupil and resource element of rate support grant achieve any significance. Where expenditure is generally high the penny rate per pupil is much higher than the national average (4·6 in this cluster compared with a national average of 2·7) and the resource element of the rate support grant is 0·0 (compared with a national average of 15·5). This pattern occurs in a similar way in cluster 2, but to a lesser extent. This can largely be explained by the social-class background and plentiful resources in these areas. However, the discrepancy between the scores on these two indices for cluster 2 and cluster 4 can probably be explained by policy direction.

Although the social-class composition of such areas is largely middle class and non-manual, these authorities are likely to be poor areas, or at least contain concentrated areas of poor housing and inadequate social amenities. These authorities are largely Labour controlled and fairly industrial. The only two county boroughs in cluster 4 are Bristol and Southampton. No English or Welsh counties fall into this cluster, the remaining LEAs being London Boroughs.

CLUSTER 5

Cluster 5 contains largely rural areas, as is evidenced by the large proportion of manual occupations and low density of population. The social-class background of such areas is typically mixed and the pattern of housing tenure reveals an average level of owner-occupation. However, the provision of social amenities for such areas is below average.

These Conservative controlled authorities support a selective system of secondary education with a large proportion of secondary modern schools. In addition to grammar schools, such areas also offer places in grant-aided and independent schools. This pattern of provision reflects the mixed social-class background of many rural areas. The pattern of expenditure throughout primary and secondary education is marginally below average.

The attainment rates of authorities in cluster 5 are below

average, both for rates of staying on beyond the statutory minimum leaving age and for awards to further and higher education, with the exception of lesser value awards and teacher training awards, which are above average.

The LEAs falling into cluster 5 include Barrow, Blackpool, Exeter, Leeds, York, Yorks W. Riding, and most English County Boroughs.

CLUSTER 6

Cluster 6 is comprised exclusively of Welsh counties, which are largely rural.

Such areas have an unusual class composition of above average high and low social-class populations and below average middle-class population. However, the preponderance of manual occupations combined with the low industrialisation index and very low population density provides a composite picture of rural Wales. Although the proportion of owner-occupiers is above average, other indices of housing tenure and housing conditions suggest only average provision of general social amenities.

The traditional emphasis upon education is reflected in the exceptionally high quality of provision. Although higher expenditure always occurs in secondary education, the figures for primary provision in this cluster are proportionately high. Similarly, expenditure on teachers' salaries is very high.

Another unusual feature of this cluster is the combination of comprehensive and grammar school provision. Whilst comprehensive provision is quite substantial it is not as high as in clusters 3 and 4. This pattern of provision in many cases will be due largely to the incomplete programmes of comprehensive reorganisation.

This high provision and generous pattern of expenditure sustains exceptionally high rates of attainment. The pattern of attainment is very high for rates of staying on beyond sixteen and seventeen years of age, and for awards to further education and teacher training. Awards to university, although much above the national average, are not quite as high as in cluster 2.

The Welsh counties of Breconshire, Caernarvonshire, Cardiganshire, Carmarthenshire, Merioneth, Montgomeryshire, Pembrokeshire and Radnorshire comprise cluster 6.

We now present an individual account of a representative authority for each of the six clusters.

Table 5.2
SOCIAL CLASS COMPOSITION OF AREA (PERCENTAGE OF
ECONOMICALLY ACTIVE MALES FALLING INTO THE FOLLOWING GROUPS)

	High social class	Middle class	Low social class	Manual	Non-Manual
Blackpool	15·2	58·9	22·0	60·6	35·5
Bristol	13·4	58·0	25·6	64·0	34·0
Gateshead	9·1	59·2	30·6	75·3	23·6
Merthyr Tydfil ...	7·1	51·5	39·5	77·8	20·3
Rochdale	13·0	53·3	30·8	70·8	26·3
Solihull	32·7	54·7	12·0	43·5	55·9
Wigan	10·3	53·0	35·3	76·3	22·3
Cardiganshire ...	19·7	57·0	20·6	64·2	33·1
National average ...	14·6	55·3	26·8	65·3	31·2

Table 5.3
CHARACTERISTICS OF AREA

	Low rateable value %	Owner-occupiers %	Council tenants %	Private tenants %	Households with all amenities %
Blackpool	72·7	69·8	10·2	18·1	85
Bristol	88·7	49·0	31·1	17·9	73
Gateshead	98·2	26·0	30·4	41·8	58
Merthyr Tydfil ...	99·6	51·1	26·8	19·8	6
Rochdale	95·7	45·6	27·5	24·5	62
Solihull	65·1	72·6	12·2	12·6	96
Wigan	96·6	41·9	32·6	23·9	64
Cardiganshire ...	98·1	54·8	14·4	22·1	48
National average ...	83·5	47·9	25·5	21·8	72

Table 5.4
PROVISION

	Pupil/teacher ratio prim.	secd.	Teachers' salaries prim.	secd. (costs per pupil)	Total expenditure prim.	secd.
Blackpool ...	29·7	20·5	61·9	99·8	90·8	165·8
Bristol ...	25·3	17·1	67·6	115·7	112·3	190·1
Gateshead ...	29·1	17·0	53·7	114·7	94·3	196·7
Merthyr Tydfil	26·3	16·6	71·4	126·2	112·9	199·7
Rochdale ...	29·9	14·9	59·3	120·6	92·8	223·7
Solihull ...	26·3	18·1	62·3	108·0	104·9	183·4
Wigan ...	29·5	18·0	57·2	110·1	84·1	188·0
Cardiganshire ..	17·9	17·7	98·75	125·31	138·84	194·71
National aver..	27·3	17·8	66·3	115·2	102·4	188·2

Table 5.5
POLICY

	Thirteen-year-olds in the different school types			
	Secondary modern %	Compre- hensive %	Grammar 1 %	Grammar 2 %
Blackpool ...	72·5	0·0	27·6	26·4
Bristol	6·9	83·2	9·8	9·8
Gateshead ...	15·2	81·0	3·8	2·9
Merthyr Tydfil ...	38·2	41·9	19·9	19·9
Rochdale ...	0·4	99·4	0·2	0·1
Solihull	64·8	0·1	35·0	31·7
Wigan	76·2	0·1	21·5	21·5
Cardiganshire ...	23·6	54·8	21·5	21·5
National average ..	44·1	32·2	24·3	16·4

Table 5.6
ATTAINMENT

| | Rates of staying on | | | Uptake of awards to | | |
	16 + %	17 + %	University	FE 1 (per 1000 of a single age group)	FE 2	Teacher training
Blackpool ...	37·4	19·7	89·4	87·0	55·5	59·0
Bristol	36·3	19·4	66·8	83·1	26·3	62·4
Gateshead ...	22·8	11·6	36·8	61·5	7·1	41·0
Merthyr Tydfil ...	32·3	18·9	51·7	60·7	—	61·8
Rochdale ...	32·4	17·2	50·7	68·6	6·5	66·2
Solihull	44·5	26·9	184·6	89·9	3·2	73·8
Wigan	25·2	11·7	46·9	37·5	89·1	62·9
Cardiganshire ...	51·5	32·2	136·7	307·9	165·5	92·1
National average	33·0	18·3	71·9	72·1	25·0	57·9

MERTHYR TYDFIL

The first authority we selected to visit from cluster 1 was Merthyr Tydfil. This authority is included in cluster 1 because of its selection procedures rather than its rates of attainment. The differences between this authority and the second authority we visited from cluster 1 will become apparent.

The paradox of educational success in the depressed coalmining communities of South Wales could be dismissed as the peculiar Welsh emphasis upon education; as an escape from the pits. Much can be attributed to their industrial heritage, but many parallels in terms of class composition and industrial activity can be found in parts of England which in no way compare with the educational success of Wales.

Our experience in Merthyr Tydfil certainly confirmed the conventional explanation of this peculiar Welsh success: that the Welsh 'worship at the shrine of education'. In fact, these words were used by the education officer we interviewed. The journey to Merthyr had to be carefully planned and co-ordinated as it appears to be inaccessible from almost anywhere. After flying to Cardiff and travelling by train 'up the valley' to the end of the line, Merthyr, little surprise was expressed at the length of our journey, our mode of travel, or indeed our curiosity about the singular success of this Welsh valley – education was that important.

Associations of Nye Bevan's powerful oratory, scenes from Richard Llewellyn's 'How Green Was My Valley' and memories of the Aberfan disaster certainly coloured the image we held of the valleys. However, our expectations of a landscape scarred by a tradition of coalmining were not fulfilled as we travelled through Taff's Well, Pontypridd and Merthyr Vale to Merthyr. The redevelopment in the town itself and recent housing developments surrounding Merthyr have resulted in a blend of old and new which does not sustain the image of a community tormented by economic gloom. The education officer pointed out that Merthyr is now relatively prosperous, particularly due to a large industrial complex owned by Hoover, which provides employment for more than five thousand. He did impress upon us, however, that the economic instability of the area had played a major part in informing the emphasis upon education towards qualifications. As can be seen from Table 5.2 Merthyr is unequivocally working class, and has the distinction of having the lowest rateable value in England and Wales. The patterns of housing tenure and amenities also suggest a community devoid of luxury or privilege.

Secondary educational provision in Merthyr at present comprises four large comprehensive schools, reorganisation to a comprehensive system having been undertaken as recently as 1970. Prior to 1970 the three grammar schools, seven secondary modern schools and two Roman Catholic secondary schools operated a system of relatively easy transfer, on far less selective entrance criteria than usually characterise a selective system of secondary education.

The smallest comprehensive at present caters for just over 1,150 pupils. A large purpose-built comprehensive, Afon Taf, accommodates 1,400 pupils and was proudly described as their great educational achievement in terms of provision. All the schools have a very wide catchment area, dictated by the rural character of the area. Afon Taf would have taken the generation of children killed in the Aberfan disaster, and to a certain extent was conceived as a tribute to them. The school certainly endeavours to provide maximum facilities, the extensive provision of playing fields, and especially rugby pitches, being an obvious priority.

Bishop Hedley, the Roman Catholic comprehensive school, serves a wider area than Merthyr Tydfil, taking in pupils from Breconshire and Glamorgan. However, a catchment area system governs allocation to all four schools, although some selection on the basis of previous educational experience operates. An all through eleven-to-eighteen years system operates in all schools. The four schools offer a broad range of courses at O and A level and CSE, in relation to their size.

Another highly valued facility established by the education committee and education department is an outdoor centre in the Brecon Beacons, which has been in operation since 1971. This is seen as an intrinsic part of educational provision, the education officer describing it as an 'extension of the classroom'. We gained the impression of great community involvement in this project; Hoover contributed £20,000 towards the centre, which is used by all age ranges from primary and secondary schools. The borough also runs a special school for retarded children, and a teachers' centre, which is regarded as a valuable asset.

Primary schools similarly operate a catchment area policy on a simple geographical basis. Eight primary schools serve Afon Taf, which in turn serves the whole valley. Although Merthyr aims at a high degree of co-ordination between education and housing policy, movement of population presents certain problems as houses are demolished in one area of the borough and new housing is provided elsewhere. The problem therefore occasionally arises in some localities of primary schools being denuded of children, while others become overcrowded.

The local authority has endeavoured to establish close links between primary and secondary schools. These relationships have been enhanced since secondary education has been reorganised along comprehensive lines. Headmasters meet frequently to discuss continuous syllabuses, and pupils visit their secondary schools before entry to make the transition from a small primary school as easy as possible.

As the primary schools serve a particular area the catchment area policy also operates for the pre-primary school age group. There is pre-school provision for 50 per cent of the three-to-five years age group, with ten nursery classes attached to schools. A nursery school, plus an infant and primary school, was also provided following the Aberfan disaster, and money was obtained from the urban aid programme to establish one nursery class for each ward in the borough, on the grounds that they were areas of social deprivation. Any parent is eligible to make application for nursery places through the schools or education department.

The expansion of nursery provision and development of a relevant curriculum for those remaining at school due to the raising of the school leaving age, are considered educational priorities at present.

We are told that staffing presented few problems, especially where a conscious policy of high expenditure on teachers' salaries is pursued. Although many authorities prefer their teachers to be recruited from outside the authority, the education officer in Merthyr stressed the value of a large proportion of their teaching force being local. Where close links exist within the community, headmasters and teachers form closer relationships with pupils through knowing their families. In addition to using the teachers' centre, 40 to 50 per cent of teachers attend summer schools for courses each year.

It is difficult to assess accurately the policy direction of an LEA which values its total system of education so highly. The expenditure patterns of Merthyr have been consistently high, every possible effort being made to obtain as many real advantages as possible for the children in its schools. We attempted to explore the historical forces which underly its success, and the explanations of such apparent contradictions as extremely high expenditure in an area of such low rateable value. It is also perhaps surprising that an authority with obviously egalitarian ideals and a tradition of labour politics should not have established a comprehensive system of secondary education until recently. The education officer explained this as a quite deliberate, shrewd policy, as they were determined to obtain purpose-built schools before the re-organisation of local authority areas; which will mean competing with more areas for resources under the direction of possibly a less benign authority. We gained the impression of tremendous energy in exploiting all possibilities to maximise opportunities and levels of provision for the children of Merthyr. However, like any local authority, Merthyr experiences financial constraints upon its policy, although, where consideration for the ratepayers is likely to modify expenditure on some community facility, it is highly unlikely that expenditure on education will ever be reduced. The fact that Merthyr has continued to supply free school milk is perhaps a small gesture in itself, but it is a good indication of the steadfast manner in which it pursues its priorities.

The attainment rates for Merthyr are extremely good, both in terms of staying on beyond the statutory minimum leaving age and in terms of awards to higher and further education. Educational success such as this can in part be explained by the resources available to an authority. However, authorities with a similar social-class composition and industrial structure to Merthyr do not achieve this measure of success. We were frequently confronted with explanations of success which emphasised the self-evident importance of education. The fact that 'these valleys produced Nye Bevan', in the words of the education officer, conveyed this acceptance of the high value of educational success, just as many areas would accept failure as inevitable.

The stability and quality of local Labour politics has a significant influence upon educational success, in informing policy. However, the education officer stressed that even where the political calibre and function of local Labour groups have changed, commitment to educational values has remained constant. The radicalism and nonconformity that characterised political activity in the Welsh valleys many years ago produced the first free secondary school in Merthyr in 1908, in direct opposition to the DES. Built upon this tradition there now exists a very close relationship between the education committee and education department, where education officers are given tremendous support. In addition, close links exist within the community. Every effort is made to explain any changes in the educational structure to all concerned, bringing teachers, parents, education officers and councillors together frequently. The administration of education is conceived of as an intrinsic part of that community, as education is itself.

The picture we gained, although incomplete, was of tremendous enthusiasm and energy, consciously directed towards increasing opportunities for Merthyr's schoolchildren. This involves commitment on the part of the educational administrators, local politicians, teachers and ratepayers of Merthyr. It appears to be an unquestioning commitment, which perhaps explains why there was no apparent answer to why they succeed.

WIGAN

Wigan was another of the authorities we visited as an example of authorities in cluster 1. The characteristics of the cluster as a whole are depressing, in terms of education. The authorities in this group are, in the main, poor working-class authorities which have clung on to a selective system of secondary education. Wigan is no exception. They are authorities which have low attainment rates, low expenditure levels and few people taking up higher education awards. Again, Wigan is no exception. To understand why this is so, we need to examine Wigan itself, the pattern of school provision and the constraints on educational expenditure.

Wigan is an unfortunate town which still bears the scars of its unplanned development and of industrial depression. At the height of the inter-war depression one in three adult males in Wigan was unemployed, and unemployment from the pits superimposed itself on an already desperate housing shortage. George Orwell typified the situation this way, in direct reference to the acute shortage of housing:

> And that is the central fact about housing in the industrial areas: not that the houses are poky and ugly, and insanitary and comfortless, or that they are distributed in incredibly filthy slums around belching foundries and stinking canals and slag heaps that deluge them with sulphurous smoke – though all this is perfectly true – but simply that there are not enough houses to go round.[1]

Orwell saw Wigan as part of the industrial heart of the Empire, and of the coal miners who lived there, he had this to say: 'In the metabolism of the Western world the coalminer is second in importance only to the man who ploughs the soil.'[2] The paradox for Orwell was, of course, the glaring one, that the economic importance of the people of Wigan was not in any way reflected in their incomes or living conditions.

Wigan has changed a lot since Orwell described it in the 1930s, but there is still a bare poverty about the place which is even ingrained in its architecture. The railway station out of Wigan to Manchester – Wigan Wallgate – could not have changed much since Orwell himself used it. It still has a lunar landscape of industrial dereliction, and the town's population is still exceptionally working class, as can be seen from Table 5.2. The town itself has been under Labour party control for many years, and many of the people in Wigan (we were given a figure of 33 per cent) are Catholic.

Nearly all the houses in Wigan have rateable values of less than £100. A high proportion of people live in houses owned by the council but there are, too, a large number of owner-occupiers. Wigan is not, however, a residentially ostentatious town. The proportion of houses with all amenities is below the national average. Nearly 6 per cent of Wigan's present housing stock was estimated to be unfit for habitation in 1972 and 24 per cent of the housing stock is considered to be eligible for improvement in the period from 1972 to 1991.[3] One-third of Wigan's council housing was built before the Second World War, and the local authority has spent less on the improvements of pre-war council houses than almost all other authorities in the Greater Manchester area.[4]

The same pattern of low spending can be seen in education. In the period from 1964 to 1971 Wigan spent less per schoolchild than nearly all other local authorities in the north-west, except Bury.[5] Table 5.4 indicates that Wigan's pupil/teacher ratios are higher than the national average and expenditure on teachers is below the national average. The overall expenditure on primary education is well below the national average and there is virtually no provision in Wigan for the under-fives. The five nursery classes which are provided were financed out of the urban aid programme. Secondary expenditures are the same as the national average, although they are likely to increase in the future as Wigan's plans for comprehensive education become fully operational.

We have no way of explaining this low level of provision. One official we talked to left us with the distinct impression that some politicians in Wigan showed some kind of civic pride in keeping down expenditure. We have no way of investigating this possibility. The Director of Education did inform us, however, that one of his predecessors as director would not allow teachers to go on refresher courses and that before comprehensivisation levels of financial provision for education were low. Certainly, in the minds of some people in the town, education services are thought to be deprived of resources. A pupil from one of the town's secondary schools (formerly a grammar school) told us that her mathematics exercise books were used twice, first with pencil and then subsequently with ink, in an effort to cut down on the consumption of stationery. This is, of course, a very isolated piece of information, but the same pupil went on to elaborate on other examples of the careful management of school resources. The Director of Education did point out, however, that he had to delay the plan for comprehensive reform for lack of funds. These observations may not amount to much but they do at least indicate the paucity of money provided for education in the town.

In addition we gained the distinct impression that the Education Department has, until recently at least, exerted tight controls on school expenditure. Schools can now (i.e. since the appointment of the present director) spend up to £50 before requiring the financial sanction of the authority. Before that time all school expenditure had to be agreed by the education office.

Wigan only recently adopted a comprehensive plan of secondary education. The borough had formerly operated a selective system using four grammar schools. The Director of Education underlined for us the fact that people in Wigan were proud of the grammar schools and that the teachers of Wigan were, initially, opposed to comprehensive reorganisation. In the end, too, it was the character of available school buildings which determined the kind of comprehensive education plan produced in Wigan. There are now five middle schools with an age range of ten to thirteen years, and three comprehensives for the thirteen-to-eighteen age group. The Catholic authorities in Wigan have an eleven-to-sixteen system of comprehensive schools culminating in a sixth form college. The Director pointed out that Wigan's secondary system was a difficult one to reform on comprehensive lines because of the entrenched grammar school tradition of the town. This applied particularly strongly to the

Boys Grammar School which, the Director explained, had received a disproportionate share of resources in Wigan.

In terms of policy in education it is obvious that, almost paradoxically, Wigan has pursued an elitist line, favouring in particular its selective secondary schools. It is difficult on the basis of the data and the impression we have of Wigan to work out how these aspects of Wigan's social structure we have mentioned interact to produce the low rates of educational attainment in the town. For rates of staying on at school beyond sixteen and seventeen Wigan is well below the national average. On the basis of statistics supplied to us by the Director of Education, successful candidates for university came disproportionately from one school – Wigan Grammar School. The pattern of higher education in Wigan is dominated by the large numbers of students who now receive grants for lower level courses in further education. Wigan is also typical of many working-class authorities in that awards for teacher training courses outnumber awards given for all other forms of higher education.

We left Wigan from Wallgate Station to go on to Manchester. The peeling paintwork of the railway station says a lot about Wigan. Revitalisation and renewal is just what is needed for the railway station; precisely the same is required by the town. We did wonder, however, just how far things could change in Wigan if saving money was the public virtue it seemed to be. Nor did we get the impression that Wigan was determined to pull itself up by its own educational bootstraps. Our impressions are unfortunately reinforced by the figures for educational attainment.

SOLIHULL

The local authority we selected to visit from cluster 2 was Solihull. The social-class background of areas in this cluster is clearly defined as non-manual and middle class. They are also distinguished by exceptionally high rates of attainment and generous patterns of expenditure. Solihull is typical of areas in cluster 2 and we were particularly interested in it as an area surrounded by large industrial centres.

It takes fifteen minutes to reach Solihull from Birmingham New Street Station. In that short time one is transported from a large industrial city with complex and increasing problems to what appears to be its urban antithesis, the classic suburb. The contrast could not be more stark.

Central Birmingham embraces the whole range of well-documented problems arising in part from its industrial legacy and subsequent redevelopment. Physical obsolescence and more specific manifestations of poverty such as 'twilight zones' are obvious examples. It is a noisy congested city, which can be criticised for accommodating the motor car before people. It has additional problems which are attributed to its large immigrant population.

These problems are not apparent in Solihull. Our impression was of a town whose development had been consciously planned for comfort and well-being. Its wealth was most forcefully reflected in the uniform quality of its housing. Not only were the houses large and well maintained, but were generally located in pleasant, low-density settings with an abundance of trees. The town centre blends in perfectly with the residential atmosphere. The spacious shopping precincts, though modest in architectural style, displayed none of the signs of neglect of their large city counterparts.

Solihull appears as an oasis; its planned environment cushioning it against its close proximity to large industrial centres. This apparent contrast between Solihull and Birmingham obscures a very clear relationship, one of total dependence. The large oppressive city supports the desirable suburb, providing the wealth which is realised in the plentiful resources of Solihull. Donald Read, in his book *Edwardian England*, provides a graphic historical explanation of this relationship:

> The wealthy upper middle classes had indeed passed beyond such hillsides distantly overlooking the hovels of the poor. They had withdrawn to towns and villages entirely separate from the main urban complexes, commuting by train from the Home Counties into London, from Cheshire into Manchester, from Wharfedale into Leeds. 'Like the Arab', exclaimed the Birmingham Mail in 1903, 'they are folding their tents and stealing silently away in the direction of Knowle or Solihull . . . a little revolution is in progress.'[6]

Solihull competes with many similar suburbs of Birmingham as part of a commuter belt and shares a common feature of a predominantly prosperous middle-class population. In our conversation with the Director of Education, he made it quite clear that the most useful distinction in Solihull was between upper- and lower-middle class, rather than middle and working class. The figures for class composition and housing tenure in Tables 5.2 and 5.3 provide some insight into the wealthy environment of Solihull and the areas typical of cluster 2. Another important feature of such a commuter suburb is that its largely professional and managerial workforce is highly mobile.

If, as is often quoted, education reflects society, the educational provision of Solihull mirrors perfectly the social structure of the town. Like many Conservative controlled authorities, Solihull has only just embarked upon a plan of comprehensive reorganisation, and is still in the process of change. Until now the pattern of educational provision has been selective. At present thirteen secondary schools cater for a capacity of 8,320 pupils, 2,950 attending five selective secondary schools, and 5,300 attending eight non-selective secondary modern schools.

The existence of Solihull Public School in the town, and eight other independent and direct-grant schools within easy access, has a considerable effect upon state educational provision in Solihull. Firstly, an estimated 11·1 per cent of the town's school population is catered for by some form of private education, which is a significant number when the national average is only 4·5 per cent. The local authority takes up thirty-six places per year in Solihull School and ten places per year in a Roman Catholic private school. Secondly, a more significant, but less obvious, impact of the private sector is the effect of 'scaling up' provision in schools maintained by the local authority. Where many parents could afford to pay for their children's education, but instead opt for the grammar schools, a 'pecking order' among the selective schools has emerged which gives certain schools more prestige and more able pupils, necessitating a high standard of provision, and so a self-generating process emerges. One old established girls' selective school is generally regarded as a sister school to Solihull Boys School and distinguishes itself not only by high rates of attainment, but by housing an original painting by Constable.

Such 'scaling up' of provision perhaps reduces the strict dichotomy in terms of provision between the selective and non-selective schools. The secondary modern schools benefit from a wide range of courses at examination level, thirty pupils transferring to the grammar schools each year at thirteen plus.

The affluence of the town is most clearly reflected through the fund-raising activities of the PTAS, who have provided an open air swimming pool, video equipment and other items which are luxuries rather than basic needs. Although figures for total expenditure are high, the Director stressed that Solihull operates under similar financial constraints to other local authorities, the only outstanding gesture of the corporation being £28,000 towards squash courts, which serve a dual purpose as an educational and community facility. However, where school uniform is compulsory from the age of five years, with the expense of such items as straw boaters for some parents, and where a prerequisite of parents participating in the social activities of PTAS is a dinner jacket, the lack of financial constraints upon parents certainly overcompensates for the normal constraints felt by the local authority.

Nearly all the secondary schools are housed in post-war buildings and all the schools are located in low-density residential settings, and occupy large sites. Four selective schools and one non-selective school share, with the technical college, a large campus adjacent to a landscaped park and swimming pool.

Comprehensive reorganisation will replace the present system with a new system of secondary schools for pupils aged eleven to sixteen years; a new sixth form college, catering for eight hundred initially, and the technical college will provide for the education of the sixteen to nineteen year age group. Solihull has opted for schools of eight form entry and the number of pupils will not exceed 1,200 where possible. The 11 + examination has been held for the last time this year, and children will be allocated to secondary schools on a catchment area basis, rather than by parental choice. The local authority places in direct-grant and independent schools will also cease.

Solihull's forty-two primary schools are also located on pleasant sites and the local authority is in the fortunate position of having all but seven primary schools occupying post-1945 buildings, therefore necessitating little capital expenditure on replacement of

inadequate buildings. However, the growth of the school population since the war has outpaced anticipated demand and tem-
porary classrooms are being used. An extensive building programme is also planned. Before the Plowden Committee set out
the principles for the organisation of infant and junior schools,
Solihull had adopted a system along those lines, of three form
entry junior schools, serving an area of one mile radius. The
junior and infant schools are separate and the sexes are mixed.

We were surprised to hear that the local authority provided no
pre-school education facilities. However, there are thirty-six pre-
school nursery and playgroup establishments, run on a private
basis, which cater for a large proportion of the population. The
Director regards the pre-school provision as less than adequate,
but plans submitted to the DES were turned down on grounds of
cost.

Staffing in all schools presents few problems, as the wives of
professionals living in Solihull represent a large proportion of
teachers. However, due to the high rate of mobility among the
population, the staff turnover is relatively high.

Solihull is obviously a high spender in terms of the capitation
allowance in primary and secondary schools, but expenditure on
teachers' salaries is just below the national average, which
partially reflects the availability of teachers in the area. As
Solihull possesses an adequate stock of schools and facilities, the
expenditure patterns reflect a general process of expansion, rather
than concentration of resources upon a few major projects.

Solihull's educational policy epitomises careful planning and
an absence of urgent problems, which is a feature of the town
itself. Having pursued an elitist policy of secondary education
for so long, one would expect comprehensive reorganisation to
present a complete reversal of policy and therefore considerable
problems, both in terms of negative reactions from parents and
staff, and practical difficulties such as accommodation and zoning.
However, the carefully sustained planning has enabled the
authority to avoid these problems. As the secondary schools are
envisaged as neighbourhood comprehensives with no parental
choice, grievances were expressed about discrimination against
council-house areas. The local authority responded by conducting
a socio-economic survey which revealed an adequate social mix
in these schools. Similarly, initial reactions from staff who had

taught in the selective schools for many years were negative, as they feared reallocation to schools where the curriculum was geared to a less academic level.

The close scrutiny of possible problems and the maintenance of a high quality of provision in all schools appear to have produced an educational system from which crisis and criticism are largely absent. However, it is worth noting the relative nature of what is problematic in different areas. A major concern in Solihull is the problems caused by congestion. A vicious circle has arisen in the primary schools, where the local authority has striven to reduce the need of children to cross major roads. However, as the majority of parents bring their children to and from school in cars, they present the hazard. Similarly, lack of parking space for staff and students is conceived of as a problem. These are problems born of affluence, rather than crucial problems of basic need which face other, working-class, authorities.

The elitist character of educational policy and exceptionally high standard of provision is not overtly threatened by comprehensive reorganisation. An obvious priority is catering for a sixth form population, of 640 at present, who have a record of high attainment. The new sixth form college can continue to exploit this potential and at the same time rationalise resources, which would otherwise be duplicated in secondary schools.

In our conversation with the Director there was a certain modesty and reticence about the policy direction which had resulted in such high standards of provision and attainment. He explained this success as being due largely to Solihull being 'a small intimate community' where there was a healthy degree of consultation between the Education Committee, Educational Department and the schools. We gained the impression of a town which placed implicit faith in the experts, who in turn met the demands of a largely wealthy middle-class population.

Much has been written of the self-fulfilling prophecy of failure among schoolchildren. Solihull must be an example of the self-fulfilling prophecy of success. Secondary school pupils in Solihull are expected to succeed and a very large proportion of them do. Table 5.6 reveals the exceptionally high attainment rates both in terms of staying on beyond the statutory minimum leaving age and the patterns of uptake of higher education. We were told that the average number of A Level passes in one girls' grammar school was 3·5. Indeed there is not only an elite of university candidates, but an elite of pupils gaining Oxbridge places. The route to university and subsequent desirable occupations is both carefully planned and the obvious course to take.

The impressions we gained from our brief visit to Solihull do not create an image of a town striving to increase educational opportunity in the face of many constraints. Solihull does attempt to maximise educational opportunity, and it succeeds, but it does not need to strive, nor does it suffer serious constraints. Although its policy is quite clearly elitist and its priorities well formulated, it appears to monitor the educational requirements and quietly satisfy them, rather than be a dynamic or progressive innovator.

ROCHDALE

Cluster 3 is characterised by the average quality of provision and attainment. Rochdale is typical of cluster 3 as a working-class authority with a comprehensive system of secondary education. However, it does not in any way conform to this average character of provision. We were interested in Rochdale precisely because of this nonconformity.

Like many Lancashire towns, Rochdale has retained a strong Victorian atmosphere, a quality which appears to have impressed itself upon the total environment. The journey from Manchester to Rochdale reveals a landscape scarred by obsolete cotton mills and poor housing stock. This evidence of past industrial activity, however, holds with it associations of the very origins of the Industrial Revolution and the liberal ideals which informed industrial reform. Rochdale has its roots firmly in this liberal tradition. Richard Cobden, the famous Liberal reformer, was Member of Parliament for Rochdale. It was also the founding place of the Co-operative Movement. Another important aspect of Rochdale's heritage, which is consistent with these particular aspects of Liberalism, is that of Methodism, which has exerted a marked influence in moulding the character of the town.

We gained the impression of a town which had not relinquished these ties with the past. Rochdale has a basic, unpretentious quality, appearing to fulfil its essential needs and squander little on inessential luxuries.

However, this resourcefulness must be dictated, to a large extent, by economic factors. Rochdale is a working-class town with few growth industries. It lies in a densely populated region and has felt keenly the consequences of declining industry and economic instability. Rochdale's housing problems have been documented in detail in the Deeplish Study, which estimated that there were 9,800 dwellings ripe for redevelopment between 1964 and 1981. The Deeplish Study described the housing problems of the north-west region in these terms: 'Replacement is by far the largest element of housing need. Nearly half the region's slums are in South East Lancashire where, in all, roughly 25 per cent of the housing stock is said to be in need of clearance by 1981,'[7] and added that Rochdale was somewhat worse than the regional average.

Education has obviously been one of Rochdale's priorities. Current educational provision in Rochdale is fully comprehensive, with a three-tier system of junior, middle and upper schools which has been in operation since 1970. Like many working-class authorities, Rochdale formerly had a strong grammar school tradition, but adopted the Leicestershire plan of comprehensive reorganisation in 1964, where transfer at fourteen plus was not compulsory, but by guided parental choice. Since the introduction of a fully comprehensive system in 1970, transfer from middle to upper school is at thirteen years, and children are allocated to schools on a catchment area basis.

At present there are thirty-one primary schools, eight middle schools and three upper schools, catering for approximately eighteen thousand children. There is an approximate 4 per cent annual increase in the size of the school population, which to a certain extent is due to Rochdale becoming a commuter area for Manchester.

Nursery provision has been established in the borough for quite a long time. At present 80 per cent of children aged four years and over attend 35 per cent of primary school and nursery classes, but it is intended that pre-school provision will be increased. A technical college, college of art, and centre for adult education are also maintained by the local authority, meeting the demands for further education.

A recent addition to the town's stock of educational provision, and a unique educational development in itself, is Belfield Community School, which clearly reveals the character and priorities of Rochdale's educational policy. Although Belfield School realises many of the recommendations made by the Plowden Committee it is probably the first strictly 'community' school to be established. The plans and ideas for such a school were conceived in 1969 by the Director of Education, who told us that this type of school will hopefully form the pattern of future provision in the town.

Areas such as Belfield undoubtedly exist in most towns, where large families living in poor housing are disadvantaged in most areas of their lives. The grievances of such deprived areas are rarely articulated and less often heard. Belfield School is seen as an attempt to counter the environmental handicaps which depress the life chances of children who grow up in such areas. However, the concept of community education embodied in Belfield School extends far beyond the ideas of compensatory education advanced by the Plowden Committee. Although Belfield School caters for 240 primary age pupils, it is designed to achieve far more than purely educational aims. It contains a nursery school, clinic, public library, information centre, youth centre and old people's kitchen. The centre will also be used for adult education, community meetings, social activities and indeed any use which the residents of the community decide upon. It is this decision-making aspect which makes Belfield School a radical departure from other educational experiments in deprived areas. A school council, including twenty local residents selected from every hundred houses in the area, will participate in the decision-making process and running of the centre, along with teachers and educational administrators. The Education Committee has worked closely with the Social Services Department in developing this scheme, and the Housing Department has recently undertaken a programme of revitalisation in the area. It is this concentration of resources and concerted attack upon areas of need which the Director of Education sees as a clear priority. It is the Director of Education's belief in a joint programme of action and the principle of corporate management which sustains his view that education cannot be examined in isolation.

Four more community schools have been designated for similar areas of Rochdale, and the Director hopes eventually to extend the principles of this scheme to middle and upper schools. It is hoped that such a programme can avoid or remedy the polarisation of parents and local authorities, and that by the structure of such educational provision, members of the community will become involved in the decisions which affect not only the education of their children, but have real consequences for the quality of their lives.

Expenditure upon education is seen as important and the Director believes this ultimately depends upon the willingness and demands of the public. One would expect the introduction of a community school to present a contentious political issue, if only on the grounds that there is no precedent for such a scheme by which to measure its potential success. However, educational planning does not appear to have been fraught with such problems, or to have encountered serious criticism. We were told by the Director of Education that Rochdale was an area where local representation on many issues was strong. He regarded the teaching force as achieving a desirable level of involvement in the structure of the town's educational system. Much of the teaching force is recruited locally or from other parts of Lancashire, but like many local authorities, the Director feels that there is a danger of inbred attitudes which do not permit a broad, critical view of educational and community needs.

The rates of attainment, both in terms of remaining at school beyond sixteen and seventeen years and in terms of entry to further and higher education, are average. It could easily be argued that the high level of educational provision does not 'pay off', for under selective or comprehensive systems of secondary organisation, high expenditure is regarded as an investment, producing examination successes. However, Rochdale is chiefly concerned with another self-fulfilling prophecy, that of failure. Its resources are concentrated upon halting a cycle of deprivation and thereby achieving real opportunities for a large proportion of its population, for whom education has been largely irrelevant.

When we started out, we had a generalised picture of Rochdale as a progressive working-class authority. We could not have anticipated that this description would prove to be so accurate. From the impressions we gained from the town and our discussions with the Director of Education, it is clear that the broad perspective of education and the participation which is practised in Rochdale will have far greater implications for its school-children than the educational aims of a nominal system of comprehensive education.

GATESHEAD

Another example of a cluster 3 authority is Gateshead in the north-east of England. We did not visit this authority as part of the series of visits we made as a result of the cluster analyses. We had visited Gateshead in order to collect material for an Open University radio programme, which was finally broadcast under the title 'Policies, Authority and Attainment'.[8] We include an account of Gateshead, however, since the material is readily available to us, and because the case of Gateshead illustrates rather well the kinds of historical constraints on local educational policy which underly so much of the variation in provision and attainment in England and Wales.

Gateshead is an urban borough just south of Newcastle-upon-Tyne. It was described by J. B. Priestley in his *English Journey* in 1933 as 'a huge, dingy dormitory for the working class'. In forty years Gateshead has been transformed. The town centre has been raped by the planners, and scything through the middle of it is a motorway, in some places only a few feet away from the high-rise flats Gateshead has built to solve its housing problem.

Pre-war squalor has, however, proved itself to be obstinately persistent in Gateshead, and much still needs to be done to improve Gateshead's housing stock and other amenities. As can be seen from Table 5.3, less than 2 per cent of Gateshead's houses have rateable values of more than £100 per annum, and just over half of Gateshead's houses have all amenities.

The town has a predominantly working-class population, although there are pockets of residential building which exude urban affluence. In terms of educational attainment, Gateshead must be ranked as one of the poor local authorities. As can be seen from Table 5.6, attainment rates at sixteen and seventeen are well below the national average, and so are the numbers of children going on to various forms of higher education. In this respect it might seem inconsistent that we have located Gateshead in our third cluster of progressive working-class authorities.

This cluster location is not so surprising, however, when expenditure, provision and policy variables are taken into account. A local councillor informed us that in recent times Gateshead has been one of the highest rated boroughs in the country, and that a high proportion of rate revenue has gone into clearing away slums and council rebuilding. In the field of education we were informed, this time by the Director of Education, that Gateshead has had a massive school building programme. Between 1960 and 1965 the authority constructed eleven large secondary schools, and two Roman Catholic schools were also built. For an area which has had so many environmental problems to deal with, this is in some ways remarkable. As the Director pointed out, the building programme has meant that the oldest secondary school in the borough dates from 1956.

There is some evidence of co-ordinated housing and education policies in Gateshead. A member of the Education Committee put it this way: 'It is pointless having a beautiful school and small teacher ratio for pupils if, when the children go home at four o'clock, they have to go to a slum house with no water, no bathroom and no inside lavatory. It negates any progress you can possibly make in education.'

At several points during our conversation this councillor and the Director of Education articulated what can only be described as a multiplier theory of housing and educational investment. This is the view that spending in these areas improves education facilities, life chances and attitudes, so that educational life chances of successive generations of children are improved. In terms of our provision measures, Gateshead is slightly below the national average, although the authority spends more than the national average on secondary schools. However, during the course of our interview, the Director of Education expressed the view that Gateshead now needs to spend more on primary schools than has been the case so far.

Educational policy in Gateshead is unashamedly and almost uniformly comprehensive, and the town, as far as we can gather, experienced little difficulty in going comprehensive during the mid 1960s. This was attributed entirely to the social-class composition and political texture of a thoroughly Labour controlled education committee, functioning in a thoroughly working-class borough.

Gateshead, however, has still not succeeded in overcoming the accumulated handicaps of its history, and it is not possible for the authority to spend its way out of these handicaps. Rate revenues are almost at the maximum possible level, so that additional finance is only likely to be available through the rate support grant or the urban aid programme. The pathways of opportunity in Gateshead are therefore still limited by educational underdevelopment. There is change, however, and good grounds for believing that the building programme of the 1960s and the determined attempt to overcome its historical blight will produce changes in the pattern of educational attainment.

BRISTOL

Only two English County Boroughs fall into cluster 4, which is characterised by generous patterns of expenditure and high rates of attainment. A local authority typical of this cluster which we decided to visit was Bristol. We were particularly interested in Bristol as its system of secondary education has been organised along comprehensive lines for many years.

Bristol as a whole defies any generalised description, as it presents such stark contrasts. Such diversity, however, enhances a city, and Bristol is certainly an attractive and fascinating place. Most large towns and cities comprise areas of affluence and pockets of deprivation. Such areas in Bristol are clearly demarcated and are graphically homogeneous in terms of class composition, housing stock and general amenities.

As can be seen from Table 5.2, the population is fairly evenly distributed in terms of social-class background. Bristol can be described as a working-class city, but, as the Director of Education pointed out, it could in no way be described as a depressed area. It has probably escaped the acute effects of economic depression due to its well-balanced commercial and industrial structure. With the possible exception of the British Aircraft Corporation, the large industries in and around Bristol are not susceptible to economic instability.

Education in Bristol is not only a service provided by the local authority, but a substantial field of employment in itself. The University not only provides prestige for Bristol, and endows part of the city with a splendid architectural style, it also provides a wide range of employment. However, another consequence of a town being dominated, to a certain extent, by a university, is the demands made upon its housing stock by the increased population.

The concentration and variety of educational establishments in Bristol must be unprecedented. In addition to a large poly-technic, which is the responsibility of the local authority, training colleges and two colleges of further education, there are seven direct-grant schools in the Bristol area. The Director of Education agreed that the presence of such an extensive sector of private education did to a certain extent encroach upon the state system. There has been a tradition of some of the direct-grant and independent schools offering a few free places to the local authority each year. As some form of selection and a system of parental choice operated in Bristol until 1965, these places were offered in addition to selective secondary school places, although each direct-grant school retained its own selection procedure. However, this practice of taking up local authority places is a contentious political issue, and now that the local authority is under Labour control, the free places have ceased. Every time a change in political power occurs, the policy is reversed. When these places are filled, approximately 5 to 6 per cent of the school population is taken out of the state system, which is above the national average.

Current educational provision in Bristol and the general direction of educational policy are inextricably bound together, as the present form of comprehensive education has evolved over the last twenty years. Bristol caters for a prodigious school population, and at present has twenty-five comprehensive schools. The whole outer circle of the city is fully comprehensive, but two small inner city areas are served by grammar and secondary modern schools, and have retained the 11 +. However, these areas will eventually be incorporated into the comprehensive system.

The Director of Education described the process by which Bristol arrived at this form of secondary organisation as one of meeting the clearly defined needs of a large school population.

In the post-war period expansion of educational provision was necessary, and it was felt that teachers were inhibited in recommending able pupils for grammar school education due to the lack of places. The bilateral school was seen as an obvious solution. The first bilateral schools were opened in 1954, and increased by two per year until the educational system was completely bilateral in 1965. One half of the bilateral school was non-selective, pupils being allocated places on residence criteria. The other half operated on the principle of 11+ assessment and parental choice. However, the situation had emerged by 1965 of the less able pupil gaining a place in a local school as of right, for which the more able pupil had to compete.

The transition from bilateral to comprehensive was both obvious and easily effected, the bilateral schools providing a new stock of purpose-built schools. 'Areas of prime responsibility' were established, which means that pupils attend their local secondary school as of right. Every secondary school has in effect become a neighbourhood comprehensive. In a city such as Bristol, where the class composition of different areas varies so greatly, any real degree of social mix cannot be achieved. This is often regarded as a serious drawback to a neighbourhood comprehensive system, as it can produce similar variation in the quality of provision in different areas. A system does operate whereby application can be made for a place in an alternative school to the one in the immediate locality. The Director of Education estimated that 10 per cent do apply for alternative places, and of these approximately 5 per cent are satisfied.

The Director of Education stressed that the evolution of the present comprehensive system had been governed by careful assessment of immediate needs, rather than a conscious policy governed by political considerations. However, only careful planning and foresight could produce a system begun in 1954, which caters for the educational needs of Bristol today. The Director did point out the impracticability of reversing a system of comprehensive secondary education once it had been embarked upon. The only salient drawback to this system is the eleven to eighteen system established by the bilateral schools, which has resulted in schools of mammoth proportions. Hartcliffe Comprehensive, a fourteen form entry school, is the largest in the country. The size of the schools does range, however, from ten form entry to smaller schools, depending upon the proportion of the population they serve. Course provision, similarly, varies in relation to the size of the school.

The Director expressed pride in their stock of primary and nursery schools, the local authority having always regarded this sector of education as a priority in terms of expenditure. A training college for nursery teachers is run by the local authority and the level of non-teaching ancillary staff in primary education is high. A progressive scheme of nursery education is the provision of nursery schools in high-rise housing, built by the Housing Department. We were told that a high degree of inter-Committee co-operation exists, facilitating such schemes. Approximately half the primary schools are located in post-war buildings, and operate on a catchment area basis, feeding local comprehensives.

The deliberate policy of appointing teaching staff on high scales and maintaining high expenditure on teachers' salaries is regarded as a worthwhile investment. However, Bristol is over-subscribed in terms of teachers, and few inducements are necessary. A teachers' centre, established by the local authority, provides plentiful resources for teachers in all sectors of the educational system.

The Director of Education told us that the main constraints upon educational policy were financial constraints upon building programmes, where the sheer extent of provision always presented something of a problem. However, the high level of expenditure on education reflects a willingness to spend, and implicit value placed in the educational system. Half the city's total revenue is spent on education, which establishes it as an obvious priority.

The Director was keen to stress that when the educational needs of a particular area become obvious, a carefully formulated policy for that area is designed to meet those needs, and then it is financed; rather than tailoring the needs of a particular area to fit a strict budget.

The main achievement of this system of comprehensive education is seen to be the greater opportunities and expanded provision for the less able pupil, who would otherwise have suffered under a selective system of secondary education. However, it is felt that the present system in no way extends or benefits the more able pupil, an estimated 20 per cent.

The rates of attainment for staying on beyond sixteen and seventeen years are above the national average, but awards to university are below the national figure. This could be explained as the failure of the comprehensive system to exploit the potential of more able pupils.

From our brief impressions of Bristol we cannot avoid observing the gross disparity between the affluent middle-class areas such as Clifton and Stoke Bishop and the decaying St Paul's, whose population is composed almost totally of immigrants. The educational needs of such areas will be markedly different, as will the success of the population in articulating those needs. A comprehensive system of secondary education which is adopted as an adequate solution to the needs of a large school population, perhaps falls short of the problem. Such a situation demands a total, positive commitment to a comprehensive system designed to erode the environmental factors which result in areas of such separate identity.

BLACKPOOL

The local authority which we selected for further study from those in cluster 5 was Blackpool in Lancashire. Cluster 5 authorities as a whole do not show themselves to be particularly distinguished in any field of educational attainment. Their attainment rates are very close to national means and many of them have expenditure levels below the national average figures. Blackpool is no exception, although, inevitably, it deviates from the cluster as a whole in some respects. It could not, for instance, be described as a rural area. We were particularly interested in Blackpool, however, because it is a wealthy local authority with a population notably more middle class than some of its neighbours in Lancashire. Furthermore, it has been controlled by Conservative politicians for the last twenty-six years. In this respect Blackpool is an interesting area in which to ask questions about the kinds of assumptions which influence educational decision making, in the absence of strong political opposition.

Blackpool is an unashamedly commercial place. Its position on the west coast as a holiday resort is unchallengeable and has been so for a long time. The town centre of Blackpool is totally dominated by the holiday industry, and the famous Golden Mile of amusement arcades, ice cream parlours, gambling dens and fortune tellers. It is this awesome concentration of pleasure which stamps the town and the county borough with its distinctive social characteristics.

Blackpool is a rich town which supports a large, commercial middle class of small businessmen who run the holiday industry. It is not an industrial borough, and, as a consequence of this, its working-class population is employed in tertiary sector occupations and a significant part of its working population is seasonally transient. Unemployment in Blackpool is low, particularly during the tourist season. The holiday boarding-house owner and the play-palace proprietor are an important source of the borough's wealth. The precise social-class composition of the town is shown in Table 5.2.

Blackpool is a town of owner-occupiers, and, in terms of conventional measures, the quality of housing amenities in the borough is good. Indeed, the whole borough is so uniformly affluent and comfortable, with mile after mile of well-cared-for semi-detached houses, that it is positively depressing.

The educational system of Blackpool is undergoing change. Like many other local authorities which were grouped into cluster 5, the system of secondary education in Blackpool has for a long time been selective. By September 1974 the borough will have a fully comprehensive system of secondary education based on the sixth form college principle. At the time of our interview with Blackpool's Chief Education Officer, 25 per cent of children were in selective grammar schools, although the Chief Officer did point out that 40 per cent of the secondary school population, and therefore a large number of children in secondary modern schools, were enrolled in O level examination courses. The Chief Officer pointed out, too, that approximately sixty children each year were transferred from secondary modern schools to grammar schools, which represented an average of eight children from each secondary modern school each year.

Apart from the secondary schools, there is a modern area technical college, which was built to replace the technical college within the town itself. The old technical college could not expand without eating land presently occupied by boarding houses, and for this reason, among others, of which the availability of a better site was the most important, the new technical college was sited out of town, in Bispham.

Both the Chief Officer and and Chairman of the Education Committee were clearly very proud of the technical college. It provides a wide range of courses up to and beyond A level, and has particularly good provision for hotel and catering management courses. It would be hard indeed to deny the local relevance of the technical college curriculum. The college also attempts to link some of its courses with schools in the town and while, as the Chief Officer explained, expenditure on the college had the effect of reducing expenditure elsewhere in the education service, the town was justly proud of this resource.

Pre-school education in Blackpool is not very well catered for, although plans are being developed which will change this situation. A sum of £10,000 has been allocated for this purpose for 1973 to 1974, and the programme of nursery provision is based firmly on the principle of positive discrimination. Those areas of Blackpool with primary schools in which reading ages are below age group expectations, will receive more nursery places than those areas and schools in which reading levels are considered to be satisfactory.

Unlike some local authorities, Blackpool has not had to carry out an extensive programme of new school building in recent years, although its recent educational expenditure has been quite high in relation to the new sixth form college and the technical college. The reasons for this relatively low rate of new building are a little obscure. Of major importance, however, is the fact that Blackpool has had neither a large stock of very old schools to replace, nor a problem of too many children. These are criteria which, as the Director explained to us, the DES employs in giving loan sanctions to local authorities. Some rebuilding has, of course, taken place. Three special schools have been completely rebuilt, and nearly two and a half million pounds have been spent on the secondary schools since 1966, and half a million pounds on the primary schools during the same period. There has been an increase in expenditure, therefore, in recent years. But there is no way in which Blackpool impresses itself upon the visitor as a high spending local authority. The Chief Education Officer said himself that the local authority was very sensitive about cost-benefit criteria in relation to expenditure, and very keen to make sure that rate revenues were kept within reasonable limits, consistent with the provision of adequate services. Given the expenditure levels in Blackpool as we have set them out in Table 5.4, it is quite clear what the Chief Officer means. Blackpool's expenditure on education, despite the affluence of the town, is very average and, we suspect, concentrated on secondary education services.

Blackpool's educational policy can only be described as elitist. The principle of comprehensive education has been finely tailored to achieve the same kinds of results which the selective secondary system achieved. The Chief Officer explained that Blackpool had embraced the idea of the sixth form college to rationalise teaching resources. It would be possible to offer students a much wider range of sixth form courses than would otherwise be possible in smaller, widely dispersed school sixth forms. The Chief Officer referred to a report from the Times Educational Supplement and a report by HMIS on Blackpool itself, which, he claimed, supported his views that large numbers of small sixth forms do not produce an acceptable number of students gaining, as he put it, 'Oxbridge places'. When we suggested to him that this view of sixth form education was rather elitist, or at least, could be accused of being so, he retaliated with an interesting argument about the role of the modern sixth form. What he said was that: 'We should not be ashamed of pursuing excellence. In the days when most of the world map was red, the sixth forms produced the men who ran the Empire. Now we need to look to the sixth forms to cultivate in the younger generation a sense of democratic responsibility.'

He assured us that the back-up eleven-to-sixteen comprehensive schools which would supply the sixth form college with pupils would have a carefully planned curriculum leading up to courses available in the technical college and the sixth form college. Clearly the sixth form college will provide courses leading to university. Just one part of this plan is the provision of lecture theatres in the new sixth form college, presumably to familiarise students with university learning situations.

The word the Chief Officer used in relation to the interdependence of secondary courses was 'organic'. He also assured us that the policy of making the eleven-to-sixteen schools neighbourhood comprehensives would not in any way detract from the equality of status which would be accorded to each school. The phrase 'neighbourhood school' was not one which the Director of Education was prepared to use, since it had connotations which Blackpool was unwilling to accept. Parents are in fact given a choice of the school they wish their children to attend, and approximately 80 per cent of parents are granted their first choice. Blackpool's policy, however, is to ensure that parental choice does not effectively make schools selective. While most children go to, and will go to, the secondary school nearest to their homes, a system of banding school populations by ability is designed to ensure that no one school takes in a disproportionate number of either high ability or low ability children. The Director was confident that this system – pre-occupied as it is with cognitive abilities – will be successful in achieving its aims. It remains to be seen, however, how the system will work out in practice.

The Director explained to us how, during the last eight years, some effort had been made to ensure that schools which were more disadvantaged than others would receive additional help. Accordingly, some effort has been made to refurbish older buildings, to increase capitation allowances, to send teachers on courses and to improve pupil/teacher ratios. However, from the conversation we had, it is not entirely clear whether this effort was in anticipation of the raising of the school leaving age or whether it was part of a more coherent policy of positive discrimination to back up comprehensive plans.

Blackpool's educational attainment rates are slightly above the national average, as can be seen from Table 5.6. What is remarkable, however, is the extent to which, given the social and economic character of the place, children from Blackpool do not achieve more than they do. A significant number of pupils do go on to higher education. Blackpool is above the national average in the number of maintenance awards for university education, and only just above the national figure for awards for teacher training. In this respect Blackpool's pattern of higher education output, despite the official preoccupation with excellence, is not remarkably better than some working-class education authorities.

The evidence which we have from our short visit to Blackpool is insufficient to form any firm conclusions. Blackpool is not an educationally ostentatious town. The structure of assumptions which informs its educational decision making, we feel, is unashamedly elitist, but the level and pattern of its educational expenditure is much more pragmatic. The Chief Officer took great care to impress upon us his view that, to quote, 'spreading resources breeds mediocrity' and that, increasingly, resources had to be managed in the most technically efficient way known to modern managerial practice. But in the end it is difficult to avoid the impression that educational life chances in Blackpool are sandwiched precariously between Conservative educational policy and the rating policy of Blackpool's landladies. What impressed us about Blackpool was not that it performs badly in the field of education. To claim that would be to go beyond the evidence. On the other hand, we feel that given its social composition and wealth, it would have been expected to do much better. On the basis of the evidence, however, such a view can only remain tentative.

CARDIGANSHIRE

We were unable to visit a representative of cluster 6 authorities, but we feel it is appropriate, even with very limited data, to discuss one of the more famous ones – Cardiganshire. The local authorities included in this group are on the whole Welsh, rural and educationally very successful. Cardiganshire represents the group as a whole in a dramatic way. It is a very 'Welsh' authority. Seventy-five per cent of the population can speak Welsh.[9] It is also predominantly rural. More people are employed in agriculture than in any other sector of the economy, and, perhaps significantly, the largest employers are central and local government. The largest single employer is the University College of Wales at Aberystwyth. Aberystwyth is the main urban centre of the county, and two-fifths of the whole population are concentrated in and around it.[10]

In terms of educational performance Cardiganshire is unique. For a long time it has led the Welsh league table of education, and, as Table 5.6 indicates, it far exceeds the national average figures on all the measures of educational attainment we have used in this study.

Such results are in many ways paradoxical. Cardiganshire is not a rich county. If average income is taken as a measure of local affluence, then Cardiganshire is one of the poorest local authorities in Wales. The reason for this is quite simple. As P. J. Madgwick, N. Griffiths and V. Walker put it: 'Because of the employment pattern there is a comparatively large number of people earning comparatively low wages.'[11] This is, of course, what we would expect for an agricultural area. The relatively low income level has its counterpart in the quality of housing in the county. Nearly all households have low rateable values, and only 48 per cent have all amenities.

This kind of background does not at first sight appear to be conducive to high levels of educational attainment, or such high levels of educational expenditure. Table 5.4 indicates how far Cardiganshire deviates from the national average and from other authorities visited for the purpose of this study. Several hypotheses compete with one another as an explanation of this phenomenon.

The first, and perhaps most obvious, explanation is that the social structure of the county is very conducive to high levels of educational attainment. Rural depopulation and the absence of employment opportunities may explain the development of a strong desire to achieve educational certification to guarantee employment elsewhere. Secondly, coupled with this, there is the strong tradition of religious noncomformity which persists in the area. The historical role of noncomformity has been to produce in Wales a radical and moralistic social outlook. The historian E. J. Hobsbawm has even gone so far as to suggest that: 'It [noncomformity] also brought an alternative set of social ambitions to the economic. Thenceforth the characteristic hope of the young Welshman would not be to become rich, but to become educated and eloquent.'[12] It would, indeed, be difficult to avoid the view that 'Welsh culture' places a very high value on education and that this cultural variable has, historically, played an important role in the development of Welsh education. What is not so clear, however, is precisely how this Welsh tradition works in practice.

There is some evidence that bi-lingualism affects reading

skills.[13] To a limited degree, therefore, 'Welshness' could be seen as a brake on high levels of educational performance. It may be, too, that the economic underdevelopment of Wales for reasons quite unrelated to noncomformity, has exerted a great pressure on parents to look for income opportunities outside Wales. It may, therefore, be this underlying economic factor which has resulted in such high levels of educational provision, and in the character of that provision. The Gittins Report noted that there was a much higher proportion of small primary schools in Wales than in England, and that this tendency to provide smaller schools was extended into secondary education.[14] Such small schools also have to be seen against a background of small towns and villages in which, as P. J. Madgwick *et al.* make clear, ministers of religion and teachers still have a high social standing.[15] Factors such as these do conceivably coalesce to strengthen the importance of educational institutions for working-class communities, who have for a long time expressed their radicalism in demands for education.

Good schools, a stable teaching force, gaining the respect of the population, small communities and low pupil/teacher ratios all interact with a strong tradition of noncomformity to prime the pump of educational attainment.

In the absence of an intensive local study it is impossible to disentangle the force or direction of influence of the kinds of factors mentioned. There is no doubt, however, that simple explanations of the pressure of Welsh culture are inadequate. Welsh traditions are a product of, and integral with, the social and economic structure of Wales itself, and the pattern of its social and political development.

CONCLUSION

Cluster analysis, as we have employed it in this study, is merely a way of describing data. It does not warrant the status of an analytical procedure. However, one of its most valuable features, as a descriptive process, is in imposing limits upon the data, which results in the strength of the relationships between our variables being underestimated.

We can therefore establish that a working-class background does not inevitably lead to failure, and that it is not the sole determinant of poor attainment. By suggesting the relative importance of a number of variables in producing particular patterns of attainment, cluster analysis clarifies the essential research task of unravelling the diverse relationships which can result in education success or failure. In focussing upon an LEA, the crucial influences underlying these different relationships will be the economic and political structures of an authority, which must be scrutinised in an historical context.

It is, therefore, inadequate to label an LEA 'progressive' or 'elitist' on the face value of provision. Whether by conscious policy or the contingencies of replacing physical capital, projects emerge within a local authority which attract resources and prestige, and which inevitably detract from many other facets of an LEA. The impressions we gained from our research trips confirmed the danger of categorising local authorities in this way. It is only possible to detect the thread of policy which underlies such projects, be they sixth form colleges or community schools. However, intensive local studies are required, which attempt to uncover the constraints operating upon the development of policy and the process of decision making itself. The impressionistic studies we conducted are no substitute for specific local studies, but they do present clear relationships between class background, educational provision, policy and attainment, and provide a basis from which to examine variations among local authorities which the data so often conceal. In the next three chapters we examine our data again, employing analytical procedures which are designed to clarify the ways in which our variables relate to one another.

6

THE SIXTEEN-PLUS COHORT

In this chapter we look at the relationships between rates of staying on beyond sixteen years of age and a number of other variables among different LEAs in England and Wales. The pattern of investigation will be firstly to look at the zero-order correlations of rates of staying on, for a data set covering 160 LEAs, which includes London LEAs. This data set has no information on primary school provision. We will also look at a more restricted set of 139 LEAs for which data on primary school provision are available. Secondly, we examine the relationship of educational provision with other variables, and the relationships among our educational provision variables themselves. The main core of this chapter is concerned with the simple causal models we construct by the use of partial correlational and multiple regression techniques.

THE CORRELATES OF ATTAINMENT

Table 6.1 gives all correlations which are greater than ±0.30 for our three measures of staying on beyond sixteen years for the fuller data set. The correlations with measures describing the wealth and resources of LEAs indicate that low educational attainment is correlated with the poverty of an LEA. There are fairly strong negative correlations between all three measures of attainment and 'low rateable value', and rates of staying on beyond sixteen years for boys is significantly (substantively not

111

Table 6.1

CORRELATES OF ATTAINMENT: 16+ (139 CASES)

(only correlations with a value greater than ±0·30 have been entered)

	Boys	Girls	Both
Penny rate per pupil	0·30	—	—
Industrialisation index	−0·34	−0·35	−0·36
Low rateable value	−0·41	−0·31	−0·37
Population density	−0·32	−0·47	−0·43
Labour control	−0·36	−0·35	−0·39
1961: population educational experience (males)	−0·61	−0·65	−0·66
1961: population educational experience (females)	−0·60	−0·65	−0·57
High social class	0·62	0·63	0·66
Middle social class	—	−0·33	—
Low social class	−0·56	−0·43	−0·50
Non-manual	0·65	0·54	0·62
Manual	−0·51	−0·46	−0·50
% Owner-occupiers	0·45	0·44	0·45
% Council tenants	−0·45	−0·50	−0·49
High density	—	−0·30	−0·30
Amenities 1	0·39	0·48	0·46
Amenities 2	0·44	0·34	0·41
% Secondary modern	—	−0·32	—
Pupil/teacher ratio: primary	−0·30	−0·52	−0·44
Total expenditure: primary	−0·30	0·52	0·43
Teachers' salaries: primary	—	0·54	0·45
Total expenditure: secondary	—	0·38	0·32
Teachers' salaries: secondary	—	0·37	0·32
Overcrowding 1: primary	—	−0·53	−0·42
Overcrowding 2: primary	—	−0·37	—
Overcrowding 1: secondary	—	−0·40	−0·33
% Graduates: secondary	0·44	0·58	0·53

statistically) correlated with penny rate per pupil, which is a measure of wealth. All three attainment measures are negatively correlated with degree of Labour control, over time.

The correlations between environmental factors and our measures of attainment are strong and positive. Rates of staying on for girls seem more sensitive to environmental conditions than do those for boys: This is also the case for educational provision factors. In the case of girls, the most interesting finding is that, with one exception, secondary provision factors are markedly less important than are primary provision factors. The type of school pupils attend at thirteen years is not important, except for the negative correlation in the case of girls, with proportion in secondary modern schools, which is negatively correlated with attainment. The proportion of graduates on the secondary teaching staff of the LEA is very highly correlated with attainment. Debt charges are not highly correlated with attainment, which is probably due to this variable being a poor indicator of physical capital.

The highest correlates of attainment are the proportions of those aged twenty-five plus in 1961 who left school at fifteen years or earlier. We shall subsequently refer to this variable as '1961: population education experience'. For boys, the proportion of economically active males in 'high social-class' and 'non-manual' groups is also highly correlated with attainment. Proportions in 'manual' and 'low social-class' groups are negatively correlated with attainment for all indices, but proportion in 'middle class' is negatively correlated with attainment for girls. The correlations of housing tenure patterns with attainment similarly reflect this pattern of class correlates.

Table 6.2
CORRELATES OF ATTAINMENT: 16+ (160 CASES)
(only correlations with a value greater than ±0·30 have been entered)

	Boys	Girls	Both
Penny rate per pupil	0·50	0·35	0·44
Industrialisation index	—	—	−0·31
Low rateable value	−0·67	−0·50	−0·64
Resources element: rate support grant ...	−0·31	—	—
Labour control	−0·36	—	−0·38
High social class	0·71	0·55	0·74
Middle social class	—	—	—
Low social class	−0·70	−0·49	−0·66
Non-manual	0·78	0·55	0·75
Manual	−0·65	−0·47	−0·64
% Owner-occupiers	0·48	0·38	0·48
% Council tenants	−0·53	−0·45	−0·56
Amenities 2	0·43	—	0·40
Teachers' salaries: secondary	0·34	0·33	0·39
Total expenditure: secondary	—	—	0·34

The correlations for the data set which includes London (given in Table 6.2) are broadly similar to those for the more complete data set. The major difference is the weaker correlates for rates of staying on beyond sixteen years for girls. This probably reflects

Table 6.3

CORRELATES OF PROVISION VARIABLES: 16+ (139 CASES)

	48	49	50	51	52	53	54	55	56	57	58	59	99
Penny rate per pupil	0·31	—	—	—	—	—	—	—	0·37	—	—	—	—
Resources element: rate support grant	—0·54	0·48	0·55	—	—	—	—	—	—0·60	—0·44	—	—	—
Population density ...	—0·60	—0·45	—0·54	—	—	—	—	—	0·72	0·56	0·33	—	—
Labour control ...	0·33	—	—	—	—	—	—	—	0·37	0·30	0·33	—	—
1961: population educational experience (males) ...	0·45	—0·34	—0·44	—	—	—	—	—	0·48	0·35	—	—	—0·48
1961: population educational experience (females) ...	0·40	—0·35	—0·41	—	—	—	—	—	0·41	0·31	0·33	—	—0·38
High social class ...	—0·38	—	—	—	—	—	—	—	—	—	—0·33	—	—
Middle social class ..	0·33	—	—0·33	—	—	—	—	—	0·43	0·30	—	—	—
Council tenants ...	0·33	—	—0·31	—	—	—	—	—	0·31	—	0·36	—	—
Private tenants ...	—	—	—	—	—	—	—	—	0·32	—	—	—	—
Shared Amenities ...	—0·51	0·31	0·45	—	—	—	—	—	—0·55	—0·34	—0·39	—	—

differential white collar job opportunities in Greater London, and the way in which sixth form curriculum is geared to commercial training, demanded by the labour market in that area.

THE CORRELATES OF PROVISION

Tables 6.3 and 6.4 give the correlations exceeding ±0·30 for the 'provision' variables in the two data sets. These correlations were most important for the primary provision variables. Otherwise only one measure of secondary overcrowding and 'proportion of secondary teachers who were graduates' were strongly correlated with non-provision variables. The substantively significant correlates were measures of local authority wealth, environmental factors, which were strongly correlated with measures of overcrowding, and 1961: population educational experience. One interesting correlational pattern was the positive association between good provision and 'resources element of rate support grant'.

The high correlations between provision and 1961: population educational experience is especially important. This suggests stability over long periods of time in the association between poor educational provision and poor educational performance. The more limited data set also reflects these relationships. One measure of secondary overcrowding was significantly (substantively) correlated with class and environmental variables. 'Class' was correlated with provision in the anticipated direction, but generally these correlations were not strong.

Table 6.4
CORRELATES OF PROVISION VARIABLES: 16+ (160 CASES)

			56	57	58	59	60	61
Labour control	...	...	—	—	—	—	0·34	—
High social class	...	...	—	—	—	—	−0·35	—
Manual	...	...	—	—	—	—	0·32	—
Owner-occupiers	...	...	—	—	—	—	−0·30	—
Council tenants	...	...	—	—	—	—	0·37	—
Amenities 1	...	...	—	—	—	—	−0·35	—

Table 6.5

CORRELATIONS AMONG PROVISION VARIABLES: 16+ (139 CASES)

	48	49	50	51	52	53	54	55	56	57	58	59	99
48													
49	−0·85												
50	−0·92	0·91											
51	—	—	—										
52	—	—	—	—									
53	−0·41	0·53	0·43	—	—								
54	−0·41	0·53	0·46	—	—	0·55							
55	—	—	—	—	—	0·60	0·35						
56	0·94	−0·77	−0·89	—	—	−0·36	−0·37	—					
57	0·69	−0·56	−0·65	—	—	—	—	—	0·73				
58	0·44	−0·46	−0·45	—	—	−0·50	−0·34	—	0·44	—			
59	—	—	—	—	—	−0·44	−0·30	—	—	—	0·41		
99	−0·53	0·60	0·60	—	—	0·32	0·38	—	−0·46	—	—	—	—

Table 6.6

CORRELATIONS AMONG PROVISION VARIABLES: 16+ (160 CASES)

	46	49	52	55	56	57	58	59	60	61
46										
49	−0·81									
52	—	−0·48								
55	0·49	−0·61	0·31							
56	—	—	—	—						
57	—	—	—	—	—					
58	—	—	—	—	—	0·60				
59	—	—	—	—	—	0·47	—			
60	—	—	—	—	—	−0·51	−0·34	—		
61	—	—	—	—	—	—	—	—	0·36	

CORRELATIONS AMONG PROVISION

These are shown in Tables 6.5 and 6.6. Table 6.5 is extremely interesting, revealing that poor educational provision in primary schools is strongly associated with poor provision in secondary schools, and vice versa. In other words, deprivation and affluence in education are sustained throughout school life. The high inter-correlation of primary provision variables indicates the import-ance of the teaching force in this sector. In primary schools the most crucial provision variable is teachers. Secondary provision variables are also inter-correlated but not so strongly, indicating the comparatively greater importance in this sector, as against primary education, of things other than the teaching force. Table 6.6 includes only secondary provision variables and these reflect the correlations in the more extensive data set.

CAUSAL MODELS

We now turn to the causal models which can be generated from the subsets of the zero-order correlation matrix we have just described. Our rationale for doing so and our method of constructing these models was described in the previous chapter. Our procedure involves the computation of successive multiple correlation coefficients, and the computation from these of partial correlation coefficients. Our 'order of input' is (1) provision, (2) environmental factors and (3) population characteristics. This suggests a causal model of the form:

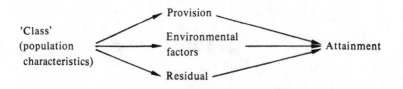

This suggests that the influence of 'class', which is a characteristic of the population of an LEA, is mediated firstly through the relationship with educational provision, secondly through the relationship with environmental factors, and lastly, through 'residual' sets incorporating the socio-cultural attributes of class groups. This model reveals clearly the predominance of provision variables. We employ eight measures of 'class':

		Variable numbers	
		Excluding London	Including London
High social class ...	...	25	33
Middle social class	...	26	34
Low social class ...	...	27	35
Non-manual	... ...	28	36
Manual ...	... ...	29	37
1961: population educational experience	(M)	23	—
	(F)	24	—
All class ...	... ...	25–29	33–37
All class + 1961: population educational experience		23–29	—

Our measures of provision, including the type of school pupils attend at age thirteen, are variables 36–59 for the extensive data set and variables 44–59 for the data set which includes London. Our measures of environmental factors are variables 16, 18, 20, 21, 33–35 (excluding London) and 26, 28, 30, 31, 40–43 (including London).

Our models are therefore built up from the following tables, which are of R^2 for sets of explanatory variables.

If we look first at the pooled relationships between rates of staying on beyond sixteen years and, successively, at educational provision, environmental factors, and educational provision plus environment factors, we arrive at Table 6.7.

For the data set including coverage of primary school provision, we can see that the pooled effect of provision variables is considerable, although much more important for girls than for boys. The importance of environmental factors is fairly constant.

Table 6.7
R^2 WITH RATES OF STAYING ON: 16+ (139 CASES)

	Boys	Girls	Both
Provision	0·36	0·57	0·47
Environmental factors	0·34	0·33	0·36
Provision + environmental factors	0·56	0·69	0·65

If we make the assumption that the effect of all common variation in provision and environmental factors can be assigned to variation in provision, then:

R^2 provision + environmental factors	$-R^2$ provision	$=$	0·20 (boys) 0·12 (girls) 0·18 (both)

For the data set covering only secondary provision the results are as shown in Table 6.8. The inclusion of London data produces some interesting findings. The response to provision for both

Table 6.8
R^2 WITH RATES OF STAYING ON: 16+ (160 CASES)

	Boys	Girls	Both
Provision (secondary only)	0·29	0·25	0·36
Environmental factors	0·52	0·32	0·51
Provision + environmental factors	0·64	0·42	0·51

boys and girls becomes much the same, and the sensitivity to environmental factors for girls is less marked. It must be stressed that provision here covers *only* secondary school provision.

When we include the effect of 'class background' variables, as listed above (p. 119), we can begin to test out our very simple causal model. We deal first and most extensively with findings relating to the more comprehensive data set (139 cases).

Table 6.9
R^2 WITH RATES OF STAYING ON: 16+ (HIGH SOCIAL CLASS)

	Boys	Girls	Both
High social class	0·39	0·40	0·44
High social class + provision	0·54	0·69	0·64
High social class + provision + environmental factors	0·60	0·72	0·69

Our measure of high social class is variable 25 as defined in the data appendix, p. 177.

R^2 high social class + provision	$-$ R^2 provision	$=$	0·18 (boys) 0·12 (girls) 0·17 (both)
R^2 high social class + provision + environmental factors	R^2 provision + $-$ environmental factors	$=$	0·04 (boys) 0·03 (girls) 0·04 (both)

If we compute the multiple-partial correlations we get the following (all values squared):

R^2 high social class; attainment: provision	$=$	0·27 (boys) 0·27 (girls) 0·30 (both)
R^2 high social class; attainment: provision + environmental factors	$=$	0·10 (boys) 0·10 (girls) 0·10 (both)

Thus the effect of 'controlling for' provision is to substantially reduce the influence of high social class upon attainment. Introducing environmental factors further reduces the influence of high social class. The multiple partials which indicate the importance of class in relation to residual variation are not large, particularly when environmental factors are taken account of. The implication of these findings is that a model of the following form is sustained by the data.

Table 6.10

R² WITH RATES OF STAYING ON: 16 + (MIDDLE SOCIAL CLASS)

	Boys	Girls	Both
Middle social class	0·02	0·11	0·07
Middle social class + provision	0·37	0·59	0·49
Middle social class + provision + environmental factors	0·58	0·70	0·67

The effect of 'middle social class' proportion of population upon attainment rates is unimportant for boys, but relatively important for girls.

R^2 middle social class + provision	$-$	R^2 provision	$=$	0·01 (boys)
				0·02 (girls)
				0·02 (both)

R^2 middle social class + provision + environmental factors	$-$	R^2 provision + environmental factors	$=$	0·02 (boys)
				0·01 (girls)
				0·01 (both)

If we compute the multiple-partial correlation coefficients:

R^2 middle social class; rates of staying on: provision	$=$	0·02 (boys)
		0·05 (girls)
		0·04 (both)

R^2 middle social class; rates of staying on: provision + environmental factors	$=$	0·04 (boys)
		0·04 (girls)
		0·03 (both)

Interpreting the effect of middle social class proportion of population is rather difficult as it exerts little influence except in the case of girls. It is clear that taking account of provision reduces the influence of class, and taking account of environmental factors further reduces that influence, in the case of girls.

Table 6.11
R^2 WITH RATES OF STAYING ON: 16 + (LOW SOCIAL CLASS)

	Boys	Girls	Both
Low social class	0·32	0·28	0·28
Low social class + provision	0·56	0·67	0·68
Low social class + provision + environmental factors	0·62	0·71	0·68

R^2 low social class + provision	$-$	R^2 provision	$=$	0·20 (boys)
				0·10 (girls)
				0·21 (both)

R^2 low social class + provision + environmental factors	$-$	R^2 provision + environmental factors	$=$	0·06 (boys)
				0·02 (girls)
				0·03 (both)

The relevant multiple-partial correlation coefficients are:

R^2 low social class; attainment: provision	$=$	0·31 (boys)
		0·20 (girls)
		0·34 (both)

R^2 low social class; attainment: provision + environmental factors	$=$	0·13 (boys)
		0·06 (girls)
		0·08 (both)

The implications of these findings are that taking account of provision much reduces the influence of low social class upon rates of staying on. Introducing environmental factors drastically reduces the importance of low social class. The multiple partials for the residual variation when provision is taken into account are quite large, but the multiple partials for class when dealing with the residual after taking account of provision *and* environmental factors, are quite small. This suggests that the role of poor environmental factors may be crucial.

Table 6.12
R^2 WITH RATES OF STAYING ON: 16 + (NON-MANUAL)

	Boys	Girls	Both
Non-manual	0·43	0·29	0·38
Non-manual + provision	0·60	0·71	0·67
Non-manual + provision + environmental factors	0·64	0·73	0·71

R^2 non-manual + provision	−	R^2 provision	=	0·24 (boys) 0·14 (girls) 0·20 (both)
R^2 non-manual + provision + environmental factors	−	R^2 provision + environmental factors	=	0·08 (boys) 0·04 (girls) 0·06 (both)

The relevant multiple-partial correlation coefficients are:

R^2 non-manual; rates of staying on: provision	=	0·36 (boys) 0·33 (girls) 0·38 (both)
R^2 non-manual; rates of staying on: provision + environmental factors	=	0·17 (boys) 0·13 (girls) 0·18 (both)

Thus taking account of provision reduces the influence of proportion non-manual upon rates of staying on, and taking account of provision and environmental factors substantially reduces it. The pattern of the multiple partials suggests that the influence of non-manual on residual variation after taking account of provision and environment is fairly small.

Table 6.13
R^2 WITH RATES OF STAYING ON: 16 + (MANUAL)

	Boys	Girls	Both
Manual	0·26	0·21	0·25
Manual + provision	0·52	0·68	0·62
Manual + provision + environmental factors ...	0·62	0·73	0·70

R^2 manual + provision   — R^2 provision   =
    0·16 (boys)
    0·11 (girls)
    0·15 (both)

R^2 manual + provision + R^2 provision +
environmental factors   —   environmental   =
    factors
    0·06 (boys)
    0·04 (girls)
    0·05 (both)

The relevant multiple-partial correlation coefficients are:

R^2 manual; rates of staying on: provision   =
    0·23 (boys)
    0·22 (girls)
    0·29 (both)

R^2 manual; rates of staying on: provision +
environmental factors   =
    0·13 (boys)
    0·12 (girls)
    0·13 (both)

The implications of these findings are that taking account of provision substantially reduces the strength of the relationship between the proportion of manual workers in an LEA and rates of staying on in that LEA. Taking account of general environmental factors even further reduces the strength of that relationship. The pattern of multiple-partial coefficients is much as previously.

Table 6.14
R^2 WITH RATES OF STAYING ON: 16 + (1961: POPULATION EDUCATIONAL EXPERIENCE)

	Boys	Girls	Both
1961: population educational experience ...	0·43	0·50	0·47
1961: population educational experience + provision	0·52	0·67	0·59
1961: population educational experience + provision + environmental factors ...	0·62	0·72	0·68

| R^2 1961: population educational experience + provision | $-$ | R^2 provision | $=$ | 0·16 (boys) 0·10 (girls) 0·12 (both) |

| R^2 1961: population educational experience + provision + environmental factors | $-$ | R^2 provision + environmental factors | $=$ | 0·06 (boys) 0·03 (girls) 0·03 (both) |

The relevant multiple-partial correlation coefficients are:

| R^2 1961: population educational experience; rates of staying on: provision | $=$ | 0·31 (boys) 0·22 (girls) 0·22 (both) |

| R^2 1961: population educational experience; rates of staying on: provision + environmental factors | $=$ | 0·13 (boys) 0·10 (girls) 0·09 (both) |

These results are extremely interesting. It has frequently been argued that a relationship exists between the class background of a given LEA and the rates of staying on at school in that authority. Such a relationship emphasises the socio-cultural aspects of class. If this model is sustained, the educational experience of the parents' generation would play a crucial role in the 'socialising environment' of those children. Parental educational experience would also have to emerge as substantially independent of variations in educational provision.

Table 6.15
R^2 WITH RATES OF STAYING ON: 16+ (ALL CLASS)

	Boys	Girls	Both
All class	0·46	0·45	0·47
All class + provision	0·65	0·72	0·70
All class + provision + environmental factors	0·67	0·76	0·73

| R^2 all class + provision | $-$ | R^2 provision | $=$ | 0·29 (boys) 0·15 (girls) 0·24 (both) |

| R^2 all class + provision + environmental factors | $-$ | R^2 provision + environmental factors | $=$ | 0·11 (boys) 0·07 (girls) 0·08 (both) |

The relevant multiple-partial correlation coefficients are:

| R^2 all class; rates of staying on: provision | $=$ | 0·43 (boys) 0·34 (girls) 0·45 (both) |

| R^2 all class; rates of staying on: provision + environmental factors | $=$ | 0·29 (boys) 0·21 (girls) 0·23 (both) |

These results are very similar to those so far obtained with the individual class measures and can be interpreted in the same way. It should, however, be noted that the size of the multiple partials is rather larger and this suggests somewhat more importance for general socio-economic class background in explaining residual variation than was the case with individual measures of that class background.

Table 6.16
R² WITH RATES OF STAYING ON: 16+ (ALL CLASS + 1961: POPULATION EDUCATIONAL EXPERIENCE)

	Boys	Girls	Both
All class ÷ 1961: population educational experience	0·55	0·57	0·56
All class + 1961: population educational experience + provision	0·66	0·75	0·70
All class + 1961: population educational experience + provision + environmental factors	0·68	0·76	0·74

R² all class + 1961:
population educational   –   R² provision   =
experience + provision

     0·30 (boys)
     0·18 (girls)
     0·25 (both)

R² all class + 1961:
population educational   R² provision +
experience + provision   –   environmental   =
+ environmental factors   factors

     0·14 (boys)
     0·07 (girls)
     0·09 (both)

The relevant multiple-partial correlation coefficients are:

R² all class + 1961: population educational
experience; rates of staying on: provision   =

     0·45 (boys)
     0·38 (girls)
     0·45 (both)

R² all class + 1961: population educational
experience; rates of staying on: provision +   =
environmental factors

     0·32 (boys)
     0·23 (girls)
     0·26 (both)

If the coefficients R² all class; rates of staying on: 1961: population educational experience are calculated, these have the values: 0·22 boys, 0·13 girls, 0·17 both.

Here, allowing for provision quite substantially reduces the impact of class background and allowing for environmental factors markedly reduces its influence.

| R^2 all class + provision
+ environmental factors
+ 1961 : population
educational experience | − | R^2 1961 : population
educational experience +
provision + environ-
mental factors | = | 0·05 (boys)
0·04 (girls)
0·05 (both) |

| R^2 rates of staying on; all class : 1961 :
population educational experience +
provision + environmental factors | = | 0·13 (boys)
0·13 (girls)
0·16 (both) |

The next regression model relates to the 160-member data set which includes London, but has a restricted coverage of provision (i.e. no coverage of primary provision).

Table 6.17
R^2 WITH RATES OF STAYING ON BEYOND 16 YEARS (160 CASES)

	Boys	Girls	Both
Provision	0·29	0·25	0·36
Environmental factors	0·52	0·32	0·51
Provision + environmental factors	0·64	0·42	0·68
All class	0·62	0·33	0·60
All class + provision	0·66	0·39	0·67
All class + provision + environmental factors	0·73	0·46	0·75

The weaker relationships with the attainment of girls reflects the reduced correlations which result from incorporating London in the data set.

| R^2 all class +
provision | − | R^2 provision | = | 0·37 (boys)
0·14 (girls)
0·31 (both) |

| R^2 all class +
provision +
environmental factors | − | R^2 provision +
environmental
factors | = | 0·09 (boys)
0·04 (girls)
0·07 (both) |

The relevant multiple-partial correlation coefficients are:

| R^2 all class; rates of staying on : provision | = | 0·52 (boys)
0·19 (girls)
0·46 (both) |

| R^2 all class; rates of staying on : provision +
environmental factors | = | 0·25 (boys)
0·07 (girls)
0·22 (both) |

When allowance is made for a restricted measure of provision, the explanatory power of 'all class' is reduced, and allowing for environmental factors reduces it further.

The major results so far are summarised in Table 6.18, which represents the difference between the squared zero-order or multiple correlation coefficient and the increment to R^2 when class variables are introduced.

Table 6.18
INCREMENTAL CHANGE AS A PERCENTAGE OF ORIGINAL R^2

		Provision	Provision + environmental factors
High social class	Boys	50	10
	Girls	30	5
	Both	39	9
Middle social class	Boys	56	100
	Girls	18	9
	Both	29	14
Low social class	Boys	38	19
	Girls	36	7
	Both	50	11
Non-manual	Boys	56	19
	Girls	48	14
	Both	53	16
Manual	Boys	62	23
	Girls	53	19
	Both	60	20
1961: population educational experience	Boys	37	14
	Girls	20	6
	Both	26	6
All class	Boys	63	24
	Girls	33	16
	Both	51	17
All class + 1961: population educational experience	Boys	55	25
	Girls	32	12
	Both	45	16
All class (160 cases)	Boys	60	14
	Girls	42	12
	Both	52	12

Table 6.18 represents the strong assumption that (1) common variation among 'class' and provision can be assigned to class, and (2) that all common variation among class on the one hand

and provision/environmental factors on the other, can be assigned to the latter set. We have argued earlier (in chapter 3) why we consider these assumptions to be justified. The clear indication from the results obtained by this method is that a model of the relationship between the social-class background of an area and the rates of staying on beyond the age of sixteen in its schools in 1970 can normally be sustained through these relationships:

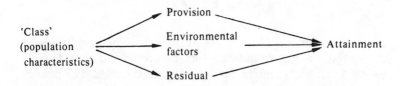

This is especially the case when the index of class background relates to the population educational experience level in the area as measured by 1961 census data.

These results will be discussed in detail in the conclusion.

7

THE SEVENTEEN-PLUS COHORT

In this chapter we look at the relationships between rates of staying on beyond seventeen years of age in different LEAs in England and Wales, and a number of other variables. The pattern of our discussion will be almost identical to that presented in the preceding chapter. Again we have two data sets, one containing 139 cases including information on the levels of primary school provision, and one comprising 160 cases for which this data was not available. We look firstly at the zero-order correlates of rates of staying on beyond seventeen years and sixteen years for this cohort. We then look at the relationship of provision with other variables, and at the relationships among our provision variables themselves. Finally we look at simple causal models.

THE CORRELATES OF ATTAINMENT

Table 7.1 gives the correlations which are greater than ±0·30 for both our measures of staying on beyond sixteen and seventeen years of age, for the fuller data set. Much the same pattern emerges as for the sixteen-plus cohort. All rates of staying on are negatively correlated with Labour control, over time. Amenity factors show strong correlations with attainment. The same general pattern of relationships between educational provision and remaining at school holds for this cohort as for the sixteen-plus cohort described in the last chapter. Again, secondary provision, with the exception of percentage of graduates in the

130

Table 7.1
CORRELATES OF ATTAINMENT: 17+ (139 CASES)

	Boys		Girls		Both	
	16+	17+	16+	17+	16+	17+
Rates of staying on: 17+ ...	0·85	—	0·91	—	−0·89	—
Labour control ...	−0·36	−0·33	−0·38	−0·32	−0·39	−0·34
1961: population educational experience (1) ...	−0·55	−0·56	−0·66	−0·60	−0·64	−0·61
1961: population educational experience ...	−0·56	−0·60	−0·59	−0·51	−0·60	−0·58
High social class ...	0·62	0·60	0·63	0·59	0·66	0·63
Middle social class	—	—	−0·33	−0·30	—	—
Low social class ...	−0·59	−0·50	−0·44	−0·41	−0·54	−0·47
Non-manual ...	0·65	0·58	0·54	0·48	0·63	0·55
Manual	−0·47	−0:38	−0·48	−0·42	−0·50	−0·42
Owner-occupiers ...	0·42	0·44	0·39	0·44	0·42	0·46
Council tenants ...	−0·43	−0·46	−0·45	−0·45	−0·47	−0·48
Amenities 1 ...	0·33	0·37	0·47	0·44	0·42	0·43
Amenities 2 ...	0·45	0·35	0·35	0·32	0·42	0·36
Secondary modern	—	−0·35	−0·35	−0·40	−0·30	−0·39
Comprehensive ...	—	—	0·31	0·30	—	—
Pupil/teacher ratio: primary ...	—	−0·40	−0·48	−0·49	−0·40	−0·47
Total expenditure: primary ...	—	0·40	0·42	0·44	0·36	0·44
Teachers' salaries: primary ...	—	0·44	0·51	0·52	0·43	0·50
Total expenditure: secondary ...	—	—	—	0·31	—	0·30
Teachers' salaries: secondary ...	—	—	0·35	0·31	—	0·30
Rates of staying on: 16+ ...	—	0·85	—	0·91	—	0·89
Overcrowding 1: primary ...	—	−0·38	−0·49	−0·49	−0·38	−0·46
Overcrowding 2: primary ...	—	—	−0·32	−0·33	—	−0·32
Overcrowding 1: secondary ...	—	−0·30	−0·44	−0·40	−0·35	−0·37
Percentage graduates: secondary	0·40	0·53	0·59	0·57	0·55	0·62

secondary teaching force, is less important than primary provision.

1961: population educational experience and social-class background variables are highly and positively correlated with rates of staying on. 'Proportion middle class' is again only important for girls. The correlation of attainment with tenure patterns broadly reflects these class correlates.

Table 7.2
CORRELATES OF ATTAINMENT: 17+ (160 CASES)

	Boys		Girls		Both	
	16+	17+	16+	17+	16+	17+
Penny rate per pupil	0·53	0·41	0·53	—	0·53	0·35
Industrialisation index	—	−0·30	—	—	—	−0·30
Low rateable value	−0·67	−0·60	−0·67	−0·51	−0·67	−0·58
Resources element: rate support grant	−0·31	—	−0·32	—	−0·31	—
Labour control ...	−0·36	−0·36	−0·36	−0·37	−0·36	−0·38
High social class...	0·72	0·71	0·73	0·71	0·72	0·74
Low social class ...	−0·71	−0·67	−0·71	−0·59	−0·72	−0·65
Non-manual ...	0·78	0·73	0·78	0·65	0·78	0·72
Manual	−0·63	−0·57	−0·63	−0·58	−0·63	−0·59
Owner-occupiers ...	0·47	0·49	0·47	0·48	0·47	0·50
Council tenants ...	−0·52	−0·53	−0·51	−0·53	−0·51	−0·55
High density ...	—	—	—	−0·30	—	—
Amenities 1 ...	0·44	0·39	0·47	0·35	0·44	0·38
Secondary modern	—	—	—	−0·30	—	—
Total expenditure: secondary ...	—	0·33	—	0·36	—	0·36
Teachers' salaries: secondary ...	0·35	0·40	0·35	0·41	0·35	0·42
Rates of staying: 16+	—	0·90	—	0·78	—	0·88
Overcrowding 1: secondary ...	−0·53	−0·53	−0·53	−0·43	−0·54	−0·50
Overcrowding 2: secondary ...	−0·44	−0·42	−0·44	−0·33	−0·44	−0·39

The pattern of correlations for the 160-case data set (see Table 7.2) is broadly similar to that for the smaller data set. Here the higher correlates of secondary provision with rates of staying on are particular interesting.

THE CORRELATES OF PROVISION

Tables 7.3 and 7.4 give the correlations exceeding ±0·30 for the provision variables in the two data sets. For the more exclusive but smaller data set (139 cases), these correlations were

Table 7.3

CORRELATES OF PROVISION VARIABLES: 17+ (139 CASES)

	72	73	74	75	76	77	78	79	83	84	85	86	99
Industrialisation index	—	—	—	—	—	—	—	—	—	—	—	—	—
Penny rate per pupil	0·31	—	—	—	—	—	—	—	−0·37	−0·44	0·35	—	—
Resources element: rate support grant	−0·54	0·47	0·58	—	—	—	—	—	−0·60	−0·44	—	—	—
Population density	0·61	−0·44	−0·55	—	—	—	—	—	0·71	0·57	0·32	—	—
Labour control	0·32	—	—	—	—	—	—	—	0·37	0·31	0·36	—	—
1961: population educational experience (1)	0·46	−0·33	−0·46	—	—	—	—	—	0·49	0·36	0·30	—	−0·50
1961: population educational experience (2)	0·40	−0·33	−0·42	—	—	—	—	—	0·42	0·33	0·36	—	−0·42
High social class	0·38	—	—	—	—	—	—	—	—	—	0·39	—	—
Middle social class	0·35	—	−0·35	—	—	—	—	—	—	0·40	—	—	—
Council tenants	0·35	—	−0·33	—	—	—	—	—	0·43	—	0·40	—	—
Amenities 1	−0·56	0·36	0·44	—	—	—	—	—	−0·58	−0·37	−0·44	—	−0·48
Secondary modern	—	−0·34	—	—	—	—	—	—	—	—	—	—	0·44
Comprehensive	—	0·38	0·33	—	—	—	—	—	—	—	—	—	—

Table 7.4

CORRELATES OF PROVISION VARIABLES: 17+ (160 CASES)

	Total expenditure secondary	Teachers' salaries secondary	Over-crowding 1	Over-crowding 2
Penny rate per pupil ...	—	—	−0·61	−0·54
Low rateable value ...	—	—	0·63	0·54
Resources element: rate support grant ...	—	—	0·36	—
Population density ...	—	—	−0·38	−0·40
High social class ...	0·30	0·30	−0·40	−0·30
Low social class	—	—	0·47	0·39
Non-manual	0·30	0·37	−0·56	−0·49
Manual	—	—	0·44	0·40

most important for the primary provision variables, otherwise only one measure of secondary overcrowding, and 'proportion of graduate teachers in the secondary teaching force', were strongly correlated with non-provision variables. The substantially significant correlates were measures of local authority wealth, environmental factors and 1961: population educational experience. Again 'resources element of rate support grant' was associated with good provision. Class background was correlated with provision in the anticipated direction, but generally these correlates were not strong, except for 'proportion middle class', which was negatively associated with provision.

The pattern in the larger, but less extensive, data set reflects the relationships of the more extensive set. The major difference is the interesting, negative, correlation between population density and degree of overcrowding, and the more marked relationship between class and provision variables.

CORRELATIONS AMONG PROVISION

These are shown in Tables 7.5 and 7.6. Again, the general pattern of provision appears to be sustained through primary and secondary school life. Primary provision variables are highly inter-correlated, whereas secondary provision is less markedly

Table 7.5

CORRELATIONS AMONG PROVISION VARIABLES: 17+ (139 CASES)

	72	73	74	75	76	77	78	79	83	84	85	86	99
72													
73	-0.84												
74	-0.93	0.90											
75			—										
76	0.31	-0.37	-0.32	—									
77	-0.33	0.40	-0.37	—	-0.52								
78	-0.33	0.40	0.41	—	-0.50	0.41							
79				—	—	0.53	—						
83	0.94	-0.76	-0.89	—	0.65	-0.30	-0.30	—					
84	0.71	-0.55	-0.68	—	0.49	-0.45	-0.48	—	0.75				
85	0.41	-0.40	-0.45	—	—	-0.30	—	—	0.42	0.30			
86				—		—		—	—	—	0.42		
99	-0.59	0.67	0.66	—	—	—	0.43	—	-0.50	-0.33	—	—	

Table 7.6

CORRELATIONS AMONG PROVISION VARIABLES: 17+ (160 CASES)

	Pupil/teacher ratio secondary	Total expenditure secondary	Teachers' salaries secondary	Debt charges secondary	Overcrowding 1 secondary	Overcrowding 2 secondary
Total expenditure: secondary ...	-0.55	—	—	—	—	—
Pupil/teacher ratio: secondary ...	—	—	—	—	—	—
Teachers' salaries: secondary ...	-0.54	0.49	—	—	—	—
Debt charges: secondary ...	—	—	—	—	—	—
Overcrowding 1: secondary ...	0.30	-0.38	-0.46	—	—	—
Overcrowding 2: secondary ...	0.40	-0.42	-0.44	—	0.89	—

inter-correlated, indicating the greater importance of the teaching force as an item of expenditure at the primary level, as compared with secondary education. Table 7.6 (160 cases) includes only secondary provision variables, and these reflect the correlations of the more extensive data set.

CAUSAL MODELS

As in the previous chapter we proceed from inspecting subsets of the zero-order correlation matrix to look at simple causal models, which can be generated from it. The general rationale behind the models and the form they take is identical to that in the previous chapter. Our measures are the same, but relate to different years of educational experience, and the variable numbers for this cohort differ slightly (see Appendix C, p. 185).

Looking firstly at the pooled relationships between rates of staying on beyond seventeen years, educational provision, environmental factors, and educational provision plus environmental factors, successively, we get Table 7.7. As in the sixteen-year-old

Table 7.7
R^2 WITH RATES OF STAYING ON: 17+ (139 CASES)

	Boys	Girls	Both
Provision	0·43	0·57	0·53
Environmental factors	0·31	0·33	0·35
Provision + environmental factors ...	0·61	0·67	0·68

cohort, the influence of provision is more marked for boys than for girls. The influence of environmental factors is comparatively constant.

For the less extensive data set covering only secondary provision, see Table 7.8.

Table 7.8
R^2 WITH RATES OF STAYING ON: 17+ (160 CASES)

	Boys	Girls	Both
Provision	0·49	0·50	0·44
Environmental factors	0·45	0·45	0·44
Provision + environmental factors ...	0·69	0·71	0·63

Again, we proceed to include 'class background' variables, and start to test out our simple causal model. We deal firstly, and most extensively with findings relating to the fuller data set (139 cases).

Table 7.9
R^2 WITH RATES OF STAYING ON: 17 + (HIGH SOCIAL CLASS)

	Boys	Girls	Both
High social class	0·36	0·35	0·39
High social class + provision	0·60	0·66	0·67
High social class + provision + environmental factors	0·65	0·74	0·71

R^2 high social class + provision	− R^2 provision	=	0·17 (boys) 0·17 (girls) 0·14 (both)
R^2 high social class + provision + environmental factors	− R^2 provision + environmental factors	=	0·04 (boys) 0·03 (girls) 0·04 (both)

The relevant multiple-partial correlation coefficients are:

R^2 high social class; rates of staying on: provision	=	0·31 (boys) 0·31 (girls) 0·32 (both)
R^2 high social class; rates of staying on: provision + environmental factors	=	0·10 (boys) 0·09 (girls) 0·12 (both)

Here allowing for provision reduces the impact of class background in a very even fashion. Including environmental factors substantially reduces the impact of class background.

Table 7.10
R^2 WITH RATES OF STAYING ON: 17 + (MIDDLE SOCIAL CLASS)

	Boys	Girls	Both
Middle social class	0·01	0·08	0·01
Middle social class + provision	0·43	0·58	0·53
Middle social class + provision + environmental factors	0·63	0·68	0·68

Thus:

R^2 middle social class+ provision	$-$	R^2 provision	$=$	0·00 (boys) 0·01 (girls) 0·00 (both)

| R^2 middle social class+ provision+ environmental factors | $-$ | R^2 provision+ environmental factors | $=$ | 0·02 (boys) 0·01 (girls) 0·00 (both) |

The relevant multiple-partial correlation coefficients are:

R^2 middle social class; rates of staying on: provision	$=$	0·00 (boys) 0·02 (girls) 0·00 (both)

| R^2 middle social class; rates of staying on: provision+ environmental factors | $=$ | 0·04 (boys) 0·03 (girls) 0·00 (both) |

Given that 'middle social class' background has a substantive influence only upon rates of staying on for girls, the general pattern of these results reveals that, when allowance is made for environmental factors, these weak relationships are further reduced.

Table 7.11
R^2 WITH RATES OF STAYING ON: 17+ (LOW SOCIAL CLASS)

	Boys	Girls	Both
Low social class	0·24	0·18	0·24
Low social class + provision	0·62	0·65	0·68
Low social class + provision + environmental factors	0·66	0·69	0·71

R^2 low social class+ provision	$-$	R^2 provision	$=$	0·19 (boys) 0·08 (girls) 0·15 (both)

| R^2 low social class+ provision+ environmental factors | $-$ | R^2 provision+ environmental factors | $=$ | 0·05 (boys) 0·02 (girls) 0·03 (both) |

The relevant multiple-partial correlation coefficients are:

R^2 low social class; rates of staying on: provision	$=$	0·33 (boys) 0·18 (girls) 0·32 (both)

| R^2 low social class; rates of staying on: provision+ environmental factors | $=$ | 0·12 (boys) 0·06 (girls) 0·09 (both) |

These results are unambiguous. Allowing for provision reduces the impact of low social class, and allowing for provision and environmental factors substantially reduces the impact of low social class. If we look at the multiple partials, it appears that the importance of low social class as a determinant of residual variation is rather larger for boys than for girls, although the importance of this is reduced when the residual over provision and environmental factors is examined.

Table 7.12
R^2 WITH RATES OF STAYING ON: 17+ (NON-MANUAL)

	Boys	Girls	Both
Non-manual	0·33	0·24	0·34
Non-manual + provision	0·64	0·65	0·68
Non-manual + provision + environmental factors	0·66	0·69	0·72

R^2 non-manual + provision	−	R^2 provision	=	0·21 (boys) 0·08 (girls) 0·15 (both)
R^2 non-manual + provision + environmental factors	−	R^2 provision + environmental factors	=	0·05 (boys) 0·02 (girls) 0·04 (both)

The relevant multiple-partial correlation coefficients are:

R^2 non-manual; rates of staying on: provision	=	0·36 (boys) 0·18 (girls) 0·32 (both)
R^2 non-manual; rates of staying on: provision + environmental factors	=	0·13 (boys) 0·06 (girls) 0·12 (both)

These results are very similar to those for the sixteen-year-old cohort and the same conclusions can be drawn.

Table 7.13
R^2 WITH RATES OF STAYING ON: 17+ (MANUAL)

	Boys	Girls	Both
Manual	0·14	0·17	0·26
Manual + provision	0·52	0·64	0·61
Manual + provision + environmental factors	0·62	0·69	0·69

				0·09 (boys)
R^2 manual + provision	−	R^2 provision	=	0·07 (girls)
				0·08 (both)

			0·01 (boys)
R^2 manual + provision + environmental factors	−	R^2 provision + environmental factors	=	0·02 (girls)
			0·01 (both)

The relevant multiple-partial correlation coefficients are:

		0·15 (boys)
R^2 manual; rates of staying on: provision	=	0·16 (girls)
		0·17 (both)
R^2 manual; rates of staying on: provision + environmental factors	=	0·03 (boys)
		0·06 (girls)
		0·03 (both)

Again, the conclusions drawn from these relationships for the sixteen-year-old cohort similarly apply to these findings.

Table 7.14
R^2 WITH RATES OF STAYING ON: 17 + (1961: POPULATION EDUCATIONAL EXPERIENCE)

	Boys	Girls	Both
1961: population educational experience	0·41	0·38	0·43
1961: population educational experience + provision	0·59	0·62	0·62
1961: population educational experience + provision + environmental factors	0·65	0·69	0·69

			0·16 (boys)
R^2 1961: population educational experience + provision	−	R^2 provision	= 0·05 (girls)
			0·09 (both)

			0·04 (boys)
R^2 1961: educational experience + provision + environmental factors	−	R^2 provision + environmental factors	= 0·02 (girls)
			0·01 (both)

The relevant multiple-partial correlation coefficients are:

		0·30 (boys)
R^2 rates of staying on; 1961: population educational experience: provision	=	0·12 (girls)
		0·19 (both)
R^2 rates of staying on; 1961: population educational experience: provision + environmental factors	=	0·10 (boys)
		0·06 (girls)
		0·03 (both)

There is a marked reduction in relationships between rates of staying on beyond seventeen years and 1961: population educational experience when we allow for provision and environmental factors. These findings reflect the similar patterns found in the sixteen-year-old cohort.

Table 7.15
R^2 WITH RATES OF STAYING ON: 17+ (ALL CLASS)

	Boys	Girls	Both
All class	0·39	0·39	0·41
All class + provision	0·67	0·69	0·70
All class + provision + environmental factors	0·68	0·70	0·73

R^2 all class + provision — R^2 provision   =   0·24 (boys)
0·12 (girls)
0·17 (both)

Therefore:

R^2 rates of staying on; all class: provision   =   0·45 (boys)
0·28 (girls)
0·36 (both)

R^2 all class; provision + environmental factors −
R^2 provision + environmental factors   =   0·08 (boys)
0·02 (girls)
0·05 (both)

Therefore:

R^2 rates of staying on; all class: provision +
environmental factors   =   0·21 (boys)
0·06 (girls)
0·16 (both)

Table 7.16
R^2 WITH RATES OF STAYING ON: 17+ (ALL CLASS + 1961: POPULATION
EDUCATIONAL EXPERIENCE)

	Boys	Girls	Both
All class + 1961: population educational experience	0·49	0·46	0·51
All class + 1961: population educational experience + provision	0·68	0·69	0·71
All class + 1961: population educational experience + provision + environmental factors	0·69	0·71	0·73

R^2 all class + 1961: population educational
experience + provision − R^2 provision   =
0·25 (boys)
0·12 (girls)
0·18 (both)

Therefore:

R^2 rates of staying on; all class: provision:
1961: population educational experience   =
0·44 (boys)
0·28 (girls)
0·38 (both)

R^2 all class + 1961: population educational
experience + provision + environmental factors −
R^2 provision + environmental factors   =
0·08 (boys)
0·04 (girls)
0·05 (both)

Therefore:

R^2 rates of staying on; all class + 1961:
population educational experience:
provision + environmental factors   =
0·21 (boys)
0·12 (girls)
0·16 (both)

Table 7.17

ALL CLASS AND RATES OF STAYING ON: 17 + (160 CASES)

	Boys	Girls	Both
All class	0·56	0·56	0·56
All class + provision	0·71	0·73	0·71
All class + provision + environmental factors	0·74	0·76	0·73

R^2 all class + provision   − R^2 provision   =
0·22 (boys)
0·23 (girls)
0·27 (both)

R^2 all class + provision
+ environmental factors   −
R^2 provision +
environmental
factors   =
0·05 (boys)
0·05 (girls)
0·10 (both)

The relevant multiple-partial correlation coefficients are:

R^2 rates of staying on; all class: provision   =
0·44 (boys)
0·46 (girls)
0·54 (both)

R^2 rates of staying on; all class: provision +
environmental factors   =
0·16 (boys)
0·16 (girls)
0·18 (both)

The relationship is greatly reduced when provision is allowed
for, especially when only secondary school provision is taken into
account. The high value of the multiple-partial coefficients is

probably an indication of the relationship between social class background and primary provision. Table 7.18 represents the ratio between the square of the zero-order correlation coefficient (or, in some cases, the multiple correlation coefficient) and the increment to R^2 when class variables are introduced. The general implication of these findings is clear. With the single exception of proportion middle social class for boys and both sexes, where the original variable had little explanatory power, incremental explanation is markedly less than original explanation. The attainment of girls is again much more sensitive to provision than the attainment of boys.

Table 7.18
INCREMENTAL CHANGE AS A PERCENTAGE OF ORIGINAL R^2

		Provision	Provision + environmental factors
High social class	Boys	47	11
	Girls	26	9
	Both	36	10
Middle social class	Boys	0	200
	Girls	13	22
	Both	0	0
Low social class	Boys	79	21
	Girls	44	11
	Both	63	13
Non-manual	Boys	63	15
	Girls	33	8
	Both	44	12
Manual	Boys	64	77
	Girls	41	12
	Both	31	4
1961: population educational experience	Boys	39	10
	Girls	13	5
	Both	21	2
All class	Boys	62	21
	Girls	31	5
	Both	41	12
1961: population educational experience + all class	Boys	51	16
	Girls	26	9
	Both	35	10
All class (160 cases)	Boys	13	9
	Girls	12	9
	Both	22	22

8

THE NINETEEN-PLUS COHORT

In this chapter we look at the relationship between the patterns of uptake of new awards for further and higher education in 1970, and a number of other variables, including educational provision, and the environmental and social-class characteristics of different LEAs. We deal only with 139 cases, for which reasonably complete data coverage of primary and secondary school provision is possible, on a longitudinally ordered basis. The data base was too restricted to make the inclusion of Greater London viable.

The strength of our provision variables for this cohort is also somewhat reduced. Small boundary changes and movements among LEAs prove to be sources of weakness in the relationship between provision during school life and rates of attainment. In addition, admission into higher education, unlike rates of staying on at school, does not always occur at a uniform age. Some new entrants would be older than eighteen or nineteen years, which makes our chronologically ordered provision variables less strongly related to attainment. Again, these factors produced a conservative bias in our general class → provision → attainment model.

The four dependent variables used in this chapter are measures of new awards to university, full value awards to further education for high level courses, lesser value awards to further education, and admission to initial courses of teacher training.

Table 8.1 presents the correlates of these variables. 'University awards' are negatively correlated with a variety of indices suggesting poor environmental conditions, and positively

Table 8.1
CORRELATES OF ATTAINMENT: 19+

	University awards	FE1	FE2	Teacher training
Industrialisation index ...	−0·46	−0·35	—	—
Low rateable value	−0·45	—	—	—
Population density	−0·35	−0·40	—	−0·37
Labour control	−0·40	−0·32	—	−0·30
1961: population educational experience 1	−0·55	−0·42	—	—
1961: population educational experience 2	−0·54	−0·40	—	—
High social class	0·72	0·44	—	0·31
Low social class	−0·58	—	—	—
Non-manual	0·72	0·31	—	—
Manual	−0·54	−0·30	—	—
Owner-occupiers	0·47	—	—	0·35
Council tenants	−0·49	−0·37	—	—
Amenities: 1	0·35	0·49	—	—
Amenities: 2	0·40	—	—	—
Overcrowding 1: primary ...	—	−0·49	−0·41	−0·33
Overcrowding 2: primary ...	—	−0·39	−0·32	—
Overcrowding 1: secondary...	−0·40	—	—	—
Percentage graduates: secd. ...	0·30	0·37	—	—
Secondary modern: (girls and total)	—	−0·37	—	—
Comprehensive: (boys) ...	—	0·45	—	—
(girls) ...	—	0·46	—	—
(both) ...	—	0·40	—	—
Grammar school 2 (boys) ...	—	—	—	0·31
(girls) ...	—	—	—	0·37
(both) ...	—	—	—	0·35
Pupil/teacher ratio: primary	−0·37	−0·33	—	—
Total expenditure: primary...	—	0·37	0·34	—
Teachers' salaries: primary...	—	0·43	0·37	—
Total expenditure: secondary	—	0·35	—	—
Teachers' salaries: secondary	—	0·43	—	—
Rates of staying on: 16+				
(boys) ...	0·42	0·40	—	0·35
(girls) ...	0·43	0·43	—	0·41
(both) ...	0·49	0·42	—	0·40
Rates of staying on: 17+				
(boys) ...	0·45	0·42	—	0·46
(girls) ...	0·47	0·42	0·32	0·46
(both) ...	0·48	0·43	—	0·48

correlated with indices suggesting favourable environmental conditions. It is predictably positively correlated with social-class background variables. University awards are correlated with three indices of provision; secondary overcrowding, graduate proportion of secondary teaching force, and primary pupil/teacher ratios.

The correlates of fuller value further education awards are broadly similar, except that this variable is more strongly correlated with provision variables. It is particularly related to the proportion of pupils in comprehensive schools at thirteen years, and is negatively correlated with the proportion of pupils in secondary modern schools.

Lesser value awards to further education are only strongly correlated with primary expenditure variables and primary overcrowding variables.

New awards for teacher training courses are positively correlated with one variable relating to favourable environmental conditions. The most interesting set of correlates which emerges for awards to teacher training is the relationship with percentage of pupils in traditional grammar schools at thirteen years, suggesting an association between elitist secondary education and entry into non-graduate teaching. As this attainment measure is not strongly correlated with measures of low social-class background, it suggests that this correlation describes to a certain extent the career structure of the working-class grammar school child. This relationship confirms earlier findings of the present authors[1] and Kelsall's findings relating to graduates of working-class origin.[2]

It is interesting to note that only university and fuller value awards in further education are strongly correlated with variables describing the social-class background of LEAs. The scarcity of strong correlations with lesser value awards reflects the highly discretionary nature of these awards, and the importance of local administrative policy in allocating them.

The pattern of correlates of provision variables is fairly predictable (see Table 8.2). In general, good provision is quite strongly associated with good environment, and rather less strongly with social-class background. Provision variables are quite strongly correlated with 1961: population educational experience. Again, the level of resources element of rate support grant is strongly associated with good provision and probably represents an index of wealthiness.

Table 8.2

CORRELATES OF PROVISION VARIABLE: 19+

	87	88	89	96	112	113	114	117	118
Penny rate per pupil	0·34	—	—	—	—	—	—	—	—
Resources element: rate support grant	-0·59	-0·43	—	—	—	—	—	—	—
Population density	-0·72	0·58	—	—	0·39	0·44	0·53	—	—
Labour control	0·38	0·33	0·36	—	—	-0·37	-0·55	—	—
1961: population educational experience 1	0·52	0·38	0·30	-0·46	0·39	—	-0·34	—	-0·37
1961: population educational experience 2	0·44	0·35	0·32	-0·38	0·30	—	-0·34	—	-0·40
High social class	-0·30	—	-0·42	—	-0·35	—	—	0·32	—
Middle social class	0·45	0·38	—	—	—	—	-0·31	—	—
Non-manual	—	—	-0·33	—	—	—	—	—	—
Manual	—	—	0·31	—	-0·30	—	—	—	—
% Owner-occupiers	-0·33	—	-0·34	—	—	—	—	—	—
% Council tenants	0·34	—	0·43	—	0·35	—	—	—	—
% Private tenants	0·34	—	—	—	—	—	—	—	—
Shared Amenities	-0·58	-0·38	-0·38	—	-0·38	—	0·40	0·32	0·31

Table 8.3

CORRELATIONS AMONG PROVISION VARIABLES: 19+

	87	88	89	90	96	112	113	114	115	116	117	118	119
87													
88	0·77												
89	0·34	—											
90	—	—	0·50										
96	−0·47	−0·30	0·34	—									
112	0·58	0·33	—	—	−0·39								
113	−0·63	−0·61	—	—	0·43	—							
114	−0·80	−0·70	—	—	0·43	—	0·90						
115	—	—	—	—	—	0·35	—	—					
116	0·30	—	0·65	0·50	0·34	—	0·32	0·36	—				
117	−0·39	—	−0·57	−0·46	0·34	−0·32	0·56	0·58	—	−0·68			
118	−0·52	−0·43	−0·48	−0·35	0·53	—	—	—	—	−0·59	0·71	—	
119	—	—	—	—	—	—	—	—	—	−0·30	0·65	—	—

The pattern of correlations among provision variables is similar to those for the sixteen-plus and seventeen-plus cohorts (see Table 8.3). In general, provision is inter-correlated and measures of primary provision are correlated with measures of secondary provision. It would appear that poor provision at five years is perpetuated throughout educational life experience.

In one respect the provision data for entrants into higher and further education are the most useful information relating to provision for all of our three cohorts, as they describe complete courses and are of necessity *not* symmetric with attainment measures. It relates to 'successful' pupils who will, in the vast majority of cases, have benefited from a full course of secondary education.

Table 8.4
R^2 WITH ATTAINMENT: 19+

	University awards	FE1	FE2	Teacher training
Provision	0·35	0·40	0·28	0·32
Environmental factors ...	0·41	0·34	0·12	0·18
Provision + environmental factors	0·63	0·53	0·35	0·38
1961: population educational experience	0·33	0·20	0·05	0·09
All class	0·55	0·24	0·08	0·10
All class + 1961: population educational experience ...	0·57	0·28	0·10	0·12
All class + provision	0·67	0·51	0·32	0·40
All class + provision + environmental factors	0·70	0·57	0·38	0·44
1961: population educational experience + provision ...	0·48	0·44	0·29	0·32
1961: population educational experience + provision + environmental factors ...	0·64	0·53	0·35	0·38
All class + provision + 1961: population educational experience	0·68	0·51	0·38	0·42
All class + 1961: population educational experience + provision + environmental factors	0·70	0·57	0·41	0·45

We now turn to our simple causal models for this cohort. For reasons of simplicity and brevity, we have employed only an 'all class' variable, and have examined the relationships between this variable and other selected variables from our data set.

Table 8.4 gives all the relevant multiple correlation coefficients.

From Table 8.4 we can see that:

R^2 all class + provision $-$ R^2 provision $=$

0·32 university
0·11 FE1
0·04 FE2
0·08 teacher training

R^2 all class + provision + environmental factors $-$ R^2 provision + environmental factors $=$

0·07 university
0·04 FE1
0·03 FE2
0·06 teacher training

Thus:

R^2 higher education; all class : provision $=$

0·49 university
0·18 FE1
0·06 FE2
0·11 teacher training

R^2 higher education; all class : provision + environmental factors $=$

0·19 university
0·09 FE1
0·05 FE2
0·10 teacher training

Similarly:

R^2 1961 : population educational experience + provision $-$ R^2 provision $=$

0·13 university
0·04 FE1
0·01 FE2
0·00 teacher training

R^2 1961 : population educational experience + provision + environmental factors $-$ R^2 provision + environmental factors $=$

0·01 university
0·00 FE1
0·00 FE2
0·00 teacher training

Thus:

R^2 higher education; 1961: population
educational experience: provision $=$

0·13 university
0·07 FE1
0·01 FE2
0·00 teacher
training

and

R^2 higher education; 1961: population
educational experience: provision +
environmental factors $=$

0·02 university
0·00 FE1
0·00 FE2
0·00 teacher
training

Finally:

R^2 all class + 1961:
population educational $-$ R^2 provision $=$
experience + provision

0·33 university
0·11 FE1
0·10 FE2
0·10 teacher
training

and

R^2 all class + 1961:
population educational R^2 provision +
experience + provision $-$ environmental $=$
+ environmental factors   factors

0·07 university
0·04 FE1
0·06 FE2
0·07 teacher
training

Thus:

R^2 higher education; 1961: population
educational experience + all class: provision $=$

0·51 university
0·18 FE1
0·14 FE2
0·15 teacher
training

and

R^2 higher education; 1961: population
educational experience + all class: provision
+ environmental factors $=$

0·19 university
0·09 FE1
0·09 FE2
0·11 teacher
training

These results are summarised in Table 8.5. Table 8.5 demonstrates that allowing for provision generally reduces the impact

Table 8.5

INCREMENTAL CHANGE AS A PERCENTAGE OF ORIGINAL R^2

		Provision	Provision + environmental factors
All class	University	58	13
	FE1	46	17
	FE2	50	38
	Teacher training	80	60
1961: population educational experience	University	40	3
	FE1	20	0
	FE2	20	0
	Teacher training	0	0
1961: population educational experience + all class	University	59	13
	FE1	39	14
	FE2	100	60
	Teacher training	83	58

of class background, and allowing for provision and environmental factors markedly reduces the impact of class background. These reductions occur for all measures of attainment, but are most marked for full value further education awards.

As people who have not passed through the state school system are differentially concentrated in higher education, and generally receive a grant, even if this is of minimum value, the findings for the relationships among class background, provision, environmental conditions and admission to universities are particularly striking.

The link is not so marked for admission to courses of teacher training, which supports an earlier contention by the authors that teacher training is the entry point into higher education for children from poor LEAS.

In the next chapter we shall examine the implications of our findings, relating to the three cohorts which are the subjects of our study.

9

CLASS, PROVISION
AND EDUCATIONAL
ATTAINMENT

In this chapter we examine the results presented in chapters 6, 7 and 8. It must be stressed at once that we are not concerned here with a general review of our findings. Neither are we concerned with a detailed exposition of the many possible types of investigation which could be applied to the data we have collected. Rather, we are pursuing our central theme; do the findings sustain the class-provision account of educational attainment set out in the early chapters of this book?

Most research in this area of study, particularly that of Coleman[1] and Jencks,[2] has centred upon the attributes of individuals and has related provision[3] to the performance of individuals. This means that comparison between our results and those generated elsewhere is very difficult in precise and exact terms.

However, we would argue that the significant implications in quantitative investigation in this type of research are general and historical, and not precise and scientific. This point is well illustrated by the grounds on which J. W. B. Douglas criticised Jencks.[4] Jencks' reanalysis of Coleman's data yielded information about individuals, and the determinants of their income and attainment. As Douglas observed, the results would have been different if the focus had been upon groups rather than individuals. Our concern has been with the relationship between class and the educational system of an advanced industrialised society. It is in terms of these relationships that the findings of individually-centred studies have usually been interpreted. We have argued that our sort of approach, using meaningful spatially defined aggregates, is a more valid method of assessing the structure of such relationships, since it looks at properties of the educational system.

The particular methodology employed in different accounts of inequality in educational systems contributes a great deal to the explanatory power of such accounts. However, comparison between such studies does not necessitate identical methodology. When we contend, for instance, that our findings contradict those of Jencks, we are not suggesting that an identical study has produced contradictory findings. Jencks has been interpreted as saying that, in advanced industrialised western societies, inequalities in school systems are not important in relation to the general structure of inequality in that society. Our findings suggest that inequalities in school systems mirror and contribute to the maintenance of the general structure of inequality in such societies.

A crucial point to be made is that the meaningful level of comparison between our study and other similar studies is the level of historical assessment of the relationship between educational systems and social structures.

SOCIO-SPATIAL INEQUALITY

Pahl's[5] exposition of the nature of the socio-spatial system is, like Rex's exposition of the nature of housing class,[6] characteristically Weberian. Both systems refer to groups which exist in relation to structures of inequality. Both groups possess sufficiently similar characteristics, as a consequence of their structural relationships, to merit consideration as classes. The crucial point is that there is no necessary link to the economically derived structure of inequality, in the Marxist sense. Ray Pahl talks about classes defined by spatial constraints. John Rex talks about classes defined by administrative constraints. Cohorts passing through schools in LEAs are defined by a combination of both.[7]

Let us then ask the question: is there a significant degree of socio-spatial inequality in the educational system of England and

Wales? Such inequality can be assessed in terms of differential outcomes (or life chances) for groups differently placed in relation to that system of inequality.

Table 9.1 gives us our answer. It consists simply of the squared multiple correlations between provision and various measures of attainment for the cohorts we described in the three previous

Table 9.1
PROVISION AND ATTAINMENT (R^2)

		All provision (139 cases)	Secondary provision (160 cases)
Rates of staying on: 16+	Boys	0·36	0·29
	Girls	0·57	0·25
	Both	0·47	0·36
Rates of staying on: 17+	Boys	0·43	0·49
	Girls	0·57	0·50
	Both	0·53	0·44
University awards		0·35	—
FE1 awards		0·48	—
FE2 awards		0·28	—
Teacher training awards		0·32	—

chapters. We would argue that the linear compound of these variables, derived from simple linear multiple regression, can be regarded as an index of spatially-defined variation in most of the system inputs into the educational experience of the cohorts studied. The output is rates of staying on at school, or rates of uptake of awards for further or higher education.

The implications of these findings are clear. Spatially-defined variations in provision are strongly related to spatially-defined variations in measures of socially significant educational attainment.

The precise way in which these relationships work in practice requires further intensive study. As we explained earlier in the book, the second part of the research project being reported here is designed to examine such relationships. In an earlier publication we suggested that a process of the kind represented in Fig. 9.1 may be operating.[8]

Figure 9.1

PROVISION-PERFORMANCE MODEL

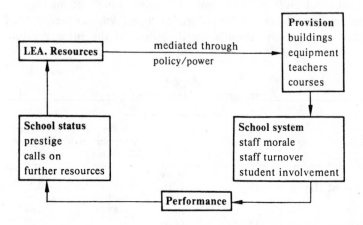

The purpose of the model was to suggest that where levels of educational provision were high and opportunities for staying on to take recognisable courses were good, then the interaction of such an opportunity structure with a committed and well-qualified teaching staff would serve to prime the pump of educational attainment. In so doing school personnel could legitimate further calls on the public purse for even higher levels of provision. Such an account is very speculative, however, and in any case can only be regarded as suggesting an explanation of only part of the variation we detect in our data. It is not implausible to suggest, however, that our provision measures do reflect social processes of the sort set out in the provision-performance model. In this respect the provision data may also reflect some measure of the subtle social interaction processes in schools which bear upon attainment and which have been so well documented in recent years.

It is at least a plausible speculation that teachers' attitudes to children and the expectation they have of children will be to some extent determined by the quality of the school, its buildings, resources and opportunities, in which they work. We are, of course, assuming here that teachers' expectations influence pupil performance in a very direct way.

In addition to a socio-spatial system of educational inequality, we have talked about the importance of general environmental factors in relation to educational attainment. There are spatial variations in general environmental conditions which have a bearing upon spatial variations in educational performance. We looked in detail at seven indices of general environmental conditions. Basically, these are indices of housing conditions and of urban industrial characteristics of localities. However, they may also represent a method of uncovering variation in the quality of the physical fabric of the schools themselves. It is not possible to measure this variation directly,[9] but if we remember the Newsom Committee's description[10] of the association between poor housing conditions and old schools (a description confirmed by the Plowden Committee)[11] then the index we employ can be considered to be, at least in part, educational. However, variations in environmental conditions are not quite so 'administrative' as variations in educational provision. Changes in education can be effected by the state and by local authorities. The role of the state in relation to environmental conditions is considerable, but not so great as in the field of education. Nonetheless we might consider its potential role to be just as great.

Table 9.2 is a repetition of Table 9.1, this time for general environmental factors, taking into account common variation among general environmental factors and educational provision. In Table 9.2 the first column for each data set gives the appropriate multiple-partial correlation^2 for environment/attainment. The second column gives the increase in R^2 when environmental factors are brought into the regression model, in addition to educational provision factors. The last column gives the multiple-partial correlation^2 for environment/attainment, taking provision into account. Table 9.2 clearly shows the importance of general environmental factors in relation to educational attainment. As we argued in chapters 6, 7 and 8, we prefer to concentrate on incremental changes in R^2. Seen from this perspective, the importance of environmental factors is clear.

The results reported above indicate a clear interconnection among measures of educational provision, measures of environmental conditions and educational attainment. Secondly, they emphasise once again the absence of territorial justice in education in this society. They also have implications in relation to the

Table 9.2
GENERAL ENVIRONMENTAL FACTORS AND ATTAINMENT (R^2)

		139 cases			160 cases		
		R^2	R^2—R^2 prov.	R^2: prov.	R^2	R^2—R^2 prov.	R^2: prov.
Rates of staying on: 16+	Boys	0·34	0·20	0·31	0·52	0·35	0·44
	Girls	0·33	0·12	0·26	0·32	0·17	0·23
	Both	0·36	0·18	0·33	0·51	0·15	0·23
Rates of staying on: 17+	Boys	0·31	0·10	0·31	0·45	0·20	0·39
	Girls	0·33	0·15	0·23	0·45	0·21	0·42
	Both	0·35		0·26	0·44	0·19	0·35
University awards		0·41	0·28	0·43	—	—	—
FE1 awards		0·34	0·13	0·22	—	—	—
FE2 awards		0·12	0·07	0·10	—	—	—
Teacher training awards		0·18	0·06	0·09	—	—	—

method of assessing the amount of central financial support for locally administered education.[12] The crucial problem to be dealt with is the relationship between the socio-spatially defined variation in educational provision (and general environmental conditions) on the one hand, and general socio-economic class on the other. The question is, do working-class children fail because they attend 'bad' schools and live in a 'poor environment', or because of the socio-cultural attributes of the class to which they belong? We wish to see if there is a strong relationship between variations in educational provision and general environmental conditions on the one hand, and variations in the social-class composition of a locality on the other. In addition we wish to know the nature of the relationship between these two background factors and educational attainment, in cohorts of pupils drawn from particular localities.

Turning firstly to the relationship of class with provision; in each of chapters 6, 7 and 8 we have included a table giving the correlates of provision. Here we look at expenditures, levels of overcrowding, and the composition of the secondary school teaching force. In every case where there is a substantial correlation between a class-background variable and a provision variable, high social class or a high level of educational experience is associated with good provision, and vice versa. This is most markedly the case for our variables describing the educational experience of the population aged twenty-five or over in 1961 in different LEAs. In the case of the other class variables, correlations with provision are not so strong, but the same general pattern is sustained without exception. The correlation matrices reveal a similar relationship between high social class and favourable environmental conditions.

The general pattern of the zero-order correlates of provision and general environmental factors is such as to sustain a model of the form of Fig. 9.2. It is important to note that this model is not directly tested out here.

The variables set out in the model are all related to one another. The patterns of variation in educational provision and in general environmental conditions are not arbitrarily imposed on the class structure in England and Wales. They are intimately and systematically related to one another and to the class structure itself.

Figure 9.2

CORRELATES OF PROVISION AND GENERAL ENVIRONMENTAL FACTORS

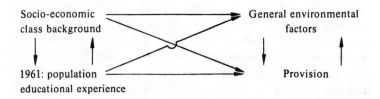

The nature of these relationships can be established by looking at the residual explanatory power of class-background variables in relation to educational-attainment variables, when provision variables and measures of environmental conditions are allowed for.

Let us look first at 1961: population educational experience. This is composed of two variables describing the educational experience of the adult population in areas outside Greater London at the time of the 1961 Census. It is not strictly a class-background variable, as it does not correspond directly to socio-economic groups, but it is particularly interesting in relation to socio-cultural explanations which we discussed in chapter 2.

One important variant of the general socio-cultural frame of reference for explaining educational inequality is the theory of the culture of poverty. Pruned to its essentials, the culture of poverty thesis states that social values and motives which run counter to dominant achievement values, and hinder the development of the latter, are passed on by parents to children in a self-reinforcing cycle. The implication of this argument is that even when opportunities, and particularly educational opportunities, are available to all children, those from a 'culturally poor' background will be unable to profit from them. Charles Valentine has criticised this approach since it fails to recognise that the attitudes and behaviour of poor people are the *results* of their position in the social structure, and not a cause of that position.[13] In relation to our analysis, the implication of the culture of poverty thesis would be that the educational experience of the general adult population of an area would be directly related to the attainment of children. Where adult educational levels are low, attainment rates will be low, and vice versa. Seen from the perspective set out by Charles Valentine, a quite different conclusion can be drawn. If parental educational experience was of under-resourced schools in poor urban areas, then the experience of the children will be similar.

Socio-cultural accounts of differential attainment do not imply any relationship between population educational experience and educational provision. The implications of our account are that, where the educational experience of the adult population was poor, schools will still be less than adequate.

At the end of each of the chapters dealing with the three age cohorts studied, we presented a table dealing with change in the explanatory power of class-background variables or variable sets in relation to attainment measures, when first provision and then general environmental conditions are taken into account. Table 9.3 gives these reductions clearly suggesting a structural model of the form of Fig. 9.3.

Table 9.3

PERCENTAGE OF ORIGINAL R^2 FOR 1961: POPULATION EDUCATIONAL EXPERIENCE (139 CASES)

		Provision	Incremental change over Provision + environmental factors
Rates of staying on: 16 +	Boys	37	14
	Girls	20	6
	Both	26	6
Rates of staying on: 17 +	Boys	39	10
	Girls	13	5
	Both	21	2
University awards		40	3
FE1 awards		20	0
FE2 awards		20	0
Teacher training awards		0	0

Figure 9.3

1961: POPULATION EDUCATIONAL EXPERIENCE, PROVISION, GENERAL
ENVIRONMENTAL FACTORS AND ATTAINMENT

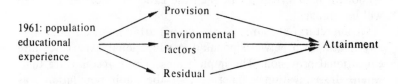

The values attached to the three modes depend on the underlying perspective. If, as we have argued above, the incremental change is most important, then the least percentage represented by the provision mode is 60 per cent and the least represented by the environmental conditions and provision modes taken together is 86 per cent. This gives a residual value of 14 per cent. The general pattern is that provision is obviously more important for girls than for boys, but environmental conditions are equally important for both girls and boys. Inspection of the relevant tables in previous chapters shows that the findings are almost identical for the larger data set including London LEAs. Thus the findings clearly support a structural conception of the relationship between 1961: population educational experience and the educational attainment of the cohorts.

Table 9.4

PERCENTAGE OF R^2 FOR ALL CLASS (139 CASES)

			Provision	Incremental change over Provision + environmental factors
Rates of staying on: 16+	...	Boys	63	24
		Girls	33	16
		Both	51	17
Rates of staying on: 17+	...	Boys	62	21
		Girls	31	5
		Both	41	12
University awards	... ...		58	13
FE1 awards	... ...		46	17
FE2 awards	... ...		50	38
Teacher training awards	...		80	60

This exercise can be repeated for all the measures of class background. In general, with the exception of proportion middle class, incremental explanation, after provision is taken into account, is less than original R^2. It can certainly be claimed that the general tendency is that taking account of provision reduces the strength of the relationship between social-class background and attainment. Taking account of both provision and environmental factors markedly reduces this relationship. This is summarised in Table 9.4.

Table 9.5

PERCENTAGE OF R^2 FOR CLASS MEASURES (139 CASES)

		Provision	Incremental change over Provision + environmental factors
High social class			
	Boys	50	10
Rates of staying on: 16+ ...	Girls	30	5
	Both	39	9
	Boys	47	11
Rates of staying on: 17+ ...	Girls	26	9
	Both	36	10
Low social class			
	Boys	38	19
Rates of staying on: 16+ ...	Girls	36	7
	Both	50	11
	Boys	79	21
Rates of staying on: 17+ ...	Girls	44	11
	Both	63	13
Non-manual			
	Boys	56	19
Rates of staying on: 16+ ...	Girls	48	14
	Both	53	16
	Boys	63	15
Rates of staying on: 17+ ...	Girls	33	8
	Both	44	12
Manual			
	Boys	62	23
Rates of staying on: 16+ ...	Girls	53	19
	Both	60	20
	Boys	64	17
Rates of staying on: 17+ ...	Girls	41	12
	Both	31	4

If we look in a similar way at the four measures of social-class background which are substantively associated with the attainment measures, then we arrive at Table 9.5.

These results are unequivocal only when we look at incremental change. The difficulty is that we have no proper measure of educational policy, other than that contained in provision itself. In chapter 4 it was suggested that certain measures might be used as indicators of egalitarian policy. The actual level of educational provision is the only real indication of commitment in this direction. The authorities in cluster 3, described in chapter 5, are all working class, but are committed to high levels of expenditure on education. In areas such as these it might be argued that, in educational terms, classes in themselves are starting to behave as classes for themselves. Cluster 6 has many of the same characteristics, suggesting that some working-class authorities are pursuing educational objectives in a big way. This means that the link between socio-economic class background and provision levels is weakened. Despite this, the results still sustain a structural account of educational attainment of the kind we have set out in Fig. 9.2.

This is particularly well illustrated in Table 9.5 by the clear reduction in the explanatory power of high social-class background when provision is taken into account.

Incremental change alone reduces the impact of high social class upon rates of staying on by at least 50 per cent. This variable is least likely to be influenced by strong commitment to educational objectives on the part of working-class LEAS. The reduction in the explanatory power of class-background variables, when both provision and general environmental factors are taken into account, is always marked and striking.[14]

Finally, in Table 9.6 we look at the relationship of attainment to all our class-background variables taken together. With the exception of two of the measures of entry into higher education, which are weakly correlated with class background to start with, the implications of these results are fairly clear. Taking incremental changes into account, the importance of our class-background variables is reduced by more than 50 per cent.

Table 9.6

PERCENTAGE OF R^2 FOR ALL CLASS-BACKGROUND VARIABLES (139 CASES)

		Provision	Incremental change over Provision + environmental factors
	Boys	55	25
Rates of staying on: 16+ ...	Girls	32	12
	Both	45	16
	Boys	51	16
Rates of staying on: 17+ ...	Girls	26	9
	Both	35	10
University awards		59	13
FE1 awards		39	14
FE2 awards		100	60
Teacher training awards ...		83	58

We maintain, then, that these results sustain a model of the following form[15].

Figure 9.4

CLASS BACKGROUND, PROVISION, ENVIRONMENTAL CONDITIONS AND ATTAINMENT

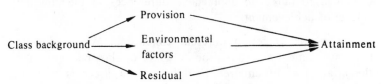

The character of the residual cannot be determined from our data. It clearly does include the social and cultural characteristics of groups of people, but it cannot refer entirely to such characteristics. The reason for this is obvious. As we have shown in chapter 5 and subsequent chapters, the kind of policy a local authority pursues influences the extent and character of what it provides. This provision, in turn, is related to measures of educational attainment. Where provision is high there is a tendency for attainment to be high. Seen from this perspective, high levels of provision can be thought of as influencing the demand for education. Certainly, when provision and environmental measures are taken into account, the importance of class-background variables by themselves is reduced significantly.

We have not attempted to examine the precise mechanisms involved in the relationship between provision and attainment for it would be almost impossible to do, given the data base for this part of our study. Nonetheless, our results so far suggest that the level of educational provision in local authority areas has a very direct bearing on educational life chances of children in those areas. In this respect, our results run counter to some recent research reports, in particular the Coleman Report in the United States.[16] For reasons which we have already set out, it is difficult to compare our results directly with other research findings. The whole tenor of much educational discussion since Coleman has been dominated by a suspicion that schools and what they provide make little difference to the educational achievement of schoolchildren. As Hodgson summarised the Coleman report, reviewing the way in which the report was received in the United States:

> When other things were equal, the report said, factors such as the amount of money spent per pupil, or the number of books in the library, or physical facilities such as gymnasiums or cafeterias or laboratories, or even differences in the curriculum, seemed to make no appreciable differences to the childrens' level of achievement.[17]

Our results suggest a different conclusion. When education and environment are equal, the influence of class background on the attainment of children in different LEA areas is markedly reduced. Such equality, of course, is rarely if ever found in practice. The argument therefore is about the mode of influence of class background upon educational attainment. Our results lead to the suggestion that the most important mode is through the structure of educational provision. In short, schools *do* matter.

In the next and final chapter we examine the implication of this argument for both educational theory and social policy in education.

10

CONCLUSION: SOCIAL POLICY, IDEOLOGY AND EDUCATIONAL ATTAINMENT

IN this final chapter we intend to review the general implications of our findings. To help us do this we return to a theme introduced in chapter 3 of this book; that is the theme of social income and the spatial pattern of its distribution.

In the light of our findings it is important that we clarify what we mean by income. Our notion of income is derived directly from Titmuss:

> No concept of income can be really equitable that stops short of the comprehensive definition which embraces all receipts which increase an individual's command over the use of a society's scarce resources – in other words, his net accretion of economic power between two points in time. . . . Hence income is the algebraic sum of (1) the market value of rights exercised in consumption and (2) the change in the value of the store of property rights between the beginning and the end of the period in question.[1]

As Harvey has observed:

> This definition has some interesting implications, one of which is that income includes change in value of an individual's property rights, irrespective of whether the change has been brought about by current addition to property which is saving in the narrow sense, or whether it has been caused by accre-

tions to the value of the property. From the point of view of the individual's command over resources, it is the change in the real value of his property which matters and not the process by which this change was brought about.[2]

The implication of these points for our discussion is not immediately obvious, but if we add to what has already been said the statement that:

> resources put into schooling are (among other things) investments in the acquisition of potential future income streams, whether looked at from the individual or societal point of view. This is a kind of capital formation. It is the formation of human capital in that the stock that will yield the future income stream is embodied in human beings . . .[3]

then, without accepting all the precise implications of the term 'human capital' we can regard the educational system and selection processes within it as being very significant for the distribution of income in society as a whole. This can only be the case, however, if it can be shown that system inputs into the education process have a causal influence upon socially significant educational attainment. These system inputs can be equated with the notion of educational social income. We use the term social income to describe income receipts which are not the consequence of participation in the labour market. In modern welfare capitalist societies, important components of individuals' incomes are transmitted through bureaucratic allocation procedures. Some of this income is in the form of cash, such as national insurance unemployment benefits and family allowances. However, a major part of this social income is in kind. Health care, local authority housing, and education can be described in this way.

Much recent research has displayed a concern with the pattern of distribution of educational social income. However, the general conclusion of this research has been that, although there is an unequal distribution of educational social income, this has implications only for the current consumption of schoolchildren. Jencks makes precisely this point when he argues for a fairer distribution of educational resources, but states unequivocally that such a redistribution would have little impact upon the subsequent income differentials among those children when they become adults.[4] The point is that we cannot equate equality of opportunity as that term is normally understood, with a fair distribution of social income, if Jencks is correct.

The question, which, in the light of Christopher Jencks' book, is still in some dispute, is how far school or system inputs to education explain differences in adult levels of income.

Writing about different definitions of inequality, Coleman has helped to clarify this issue:

> . . . a fourth type of inequality may be defined in terms of consequences of the school for individuals with equal backgrounds and abilities. In this definition equality of educational opportunity is equality of results given the same individual input.[5]

Equality of opportunity on this definition arises when all schoolchildren receive the same social income from their participation in school. Differences in attainment among individuals or groups would, on this definition, be attributable entirely to differences in intelligence or ability measured in some other way. On this definition it is important to know with some precision the contribution of the school to differences in results.

The danger in assuming that the school has little impact on differences in results is that differences then have to be accounted for in terms of the attributes of individuals. The general conclusion sustained by our findings is that school system inputs are of considerable importance in explaining differences in attainment. In addition, there is a systematic relationship between the class background of an area and the educational resources available. In general, the higher the social-class composition of an area, the better the provision. For the cohorts we studied, there was not equality of opportunity; the spatial distribution of system inputs guaranteed that school systems had different and unequal consequences for the cohorts. For them, the basic premise of the liberal approach that the system be at least equal for all has not been realised. Despite post-war educational reform, they have had to negotiate external and geographical barriers to educational success.

This accords well with Husén's recent contention that:

> The practical implication in terms of policy that ensues from

the rethinking of the concept of equal opportunity is that it is not very fruitful to put the responsibility for scholastic success or failure on the individual. One has to shift the burden of responsibility to the *system* – or to society at large.[6]

It is important, however, that this argument should be located in an historical context: 'in nineteenth century England, the idea of *equality* of educational opportunity was hardly considered; the system was designed to provide *differentiated* educational opportunity appropriate to one's station in life.'[7]

One of the prime objectives of educational policy in this country during the twentieth century has been to change the ascriptive system described by Coleman into an achievement-oriented system, organised on the basis of equality of opportunity. Simultaneously, educational policy has clearly recognised and responded to the manpower demands of the social structure. The notion of equality of opportunity has been used as a device to reconcile social justice and economic necessity.

Equality of opportunity and especially equality of educational opportunity has been a cornerstone of social democratic politics since the 1930s. In the Labour movement, as Brian Simon[8] has clearly documented, the social democratic objective of equality of opportunity had been successfully promoted as an alternative to the socialist objective of equality.

Our results demonstrate the failure to achieve equality of opportunity, even within the limited context of the state educational system, nearly thirty years after the enactment of a measure designed to do precisely that. We can detect a self-reinforcing cycle of success in the way in which the educational system functions *vis-à-vis* the labour market. Seen from this perspective, the conclusion reached by some recent French writers, that the educational system functions to reproduce the social relations of production in a capitalist society, seems inescapable. As Segré, Tanguy and Lortic put it:

> To abstract the social function of education from its economic function when postulating a direct relationship between education and production means ignoring the social and specific character of any production and changing the ideological role of any system of education.[9]

Social democratic proponents of equality of opportunity claim that it is possible to establish a situation in which the occupational destiny of a child, born into the manual working class, is a function purely of the innate ability of that child. Recently this simple position has been complicated by a concern with the alleged disabling character of a working-class socio-cultural environment. This is not a fundamental modification. In these terms compensatory education is a logical extension of the central preoccupation of those promoting equality of educational opportunity and subsequent life chances. These developments have been described in chapter 2. Our findings demonstrate that the fundamental requirement for the achievement of equality of opportunity, that is, an equal distribution of educational social income, does not exist. We ought not to be surprised by this, as Husén has said: 'The school cannot at the same time serve as an equaliser and as an instrument that establishes, reinforces and legitimizes distinctions.'[10] The educational system was not really intended to achieve social equality in the distribution of income, outside those limits set by the economic logic of the labour market. Once again the assessment of the impact of attempted reform must be, as Tawney once said, 'You can peel an onion leaf by leaf, but you cannot skin a live tiger claw by claw.'

Seen from this perspective, the persistent concern with equality of educational opportunity can only be seen as a device for obscuring the relationship between education and fundamental inequality. Equality of opportunity has served as a legitimising account of education, both for those who operate the educational system and those who are affected by it. This argument in no way detracts from the importance of an unequal distribution of educational social income. To say that it is impossible to achieve equality in education, in an otherwise fundamentally unequal society, does not mean that inequalities in education become unimportant. They are a part of, and contribute to, the general structure of inequality, just as that general structure maintains them.

POLiCY IMPLICATIONS

What our research consisted of was, in a sense, a social audit of the educational system of England and Wales, where we attempted to assess its impact on the educational careers of three cohorts of children. This audit comes about almost thirty years after an Education Act designed to achieve equality of opportunity. What the study revealed was territorial injustice and the strong effect which such injustice has in explaining social-class differences in educational attainment.

In terms of practical social policy the first and most important implication of our findings is that there should be greater equality in the distribution of educational resources. In furtherance of this aim, it is important that there should be a continuous social audit of the state of the educational social income distribution, and that information drawn from it be made easily available to the public at large. If there is, as we contend, an educational income distribution, then those who are affected by it ought to know about it. The principle 'to those that have, it shall be given' operates very clearly in education. All that we are recommending is that those who have not should be encouraged to shout about it. What we are suggesting is that people should attempt to get their rights and, in the course of doing so, develop a political understanding of the nature of the processes which affect their lives.

Applied to education this argument amounts to no more than a demand that people be encouraged to press, as of right, for those resources which directly influence educational opportunities to be made available to all groups of children. It would indeed be a tragedy if legitimate political pressure to press for such equality of resource distribution were diverted by an argument that resources and patterns of provision were relatively insignificant for educational attainment.

We may appear to be advancing a contradictory argument. We have spent the first half of this chapter suggesting that an equal distribution of educational social income is impossible in the kind of society in which we live, yet we are suggesting that people should demand such equality. Our position is very similar to that of the Claimants Unions in this country in relation to the social security system. The Claimants Unions lend no support whatsoever and, indeed, are opposed to, the social system of welfare capitalism within which they function. Their position is that welfare capitalism makes promises which it cannot keep. In the context of social security this means that claimants cannot be given all that they appear to be entitled to, nor be treated as well as legislation suggests they ought to be. These groups aim to organise claimants to maximise the uptake of welfare benefits. At the same time, they see the main gain in terms of the development of a political consciousness. People come to realise the real nature of the social security system and its function in maintaining capitalist society. Simultaneously, they come to appreciate the importance of an organisation in challenging the systems which affect them.

We suggest that what is required is for radical teachers and parents groups to come together and make demands of the educational services in their areas in the same way, and for the same reasons, as Claimants Unions organise around and make demands of the social security system. In the short run such demands may very well be for extensive policies of positive discrimination. In this respect we agree with the recommendation of the Plowden Committee that: 'Schools in deprived areas should be given priority in many respects. The first step must be to raise schools with low standards to the national average; the second, quite deliberately to make them better.'[11] We cannot agree, however, with the rationale behind this particular suggestion or the practical consequences which flow from it.

The rationale for positive discrimination was put this way by the Plowden Committee.

> The proposition that good schools should make up for a poor environment is far from new. It derives from the notion that there should be equality of opportunity for all, but recognises that children in some districts will only get the same opportunity as those who live elsewhere if they have unequally generous treatment. It was accepted before the First World War that some children could not be effectively taught until they had been properly fed. Hence free meals were provided. Today their need is for enriched intellectual nourishment. Planned and positive discrimination in favour of deprived areas could bring about an advance in the education of children in the 1970s as great as the advance in their nutrition to which school meals and milk contributed so much.[12]

We would contend, on the other hand, that the focus of positive discrimination, tied as it is to some notion of intellectual nourishment, is wrong. It is not intellectual nourishment in the school, as a compensation for lack of it in the home, which working-class children require. It is additional educational facilities as *short-term* compensation for the poor condition of the houses in which they live, and the areas in which those houses are located. The problems of urban deprivation which community educationalists have to face are the accumulated debris of years of neglect, economic change, poverty and powerlessness.

We have not set out to produce a detailed programme for educational reform, either at a local or national level. The audience which concerns us is not those who control the educational system. We direct our remarks chiefly to practising teachers, student teachers, community workers and social workers, and hopefully, through them, to the parents and children who are discriminated against by the present system. It seems to us that most radical proposals for education are directed at teachers and what they teach. We do not in any way deny the importance of overt and hidden curricula as control mechanisms and stratifying devices in our society. A preoccupation with curriculum is not, we suggest, the best basis upon which to forge an alliance between radical teachers and working-class parents and children. Both teachers in working-class areas and the parents and children living in those areas are adversely affected by the existing system of the distribution of educational social income. They can unite in demanding more. Such demands are intrinsically open-ended. Inequalities in provision are measurable and comprehensible. Organisation around these simple issues serves as a process of political education and may contribute to the development of a political base to challenge more complex educational issues and the fundamental structure of inequality.

We hope that this book reinforces the demands of those people in society who are pressing for change, and who cannot see the logic of continuing to blame poverty on the poor.

We referred at the beginning of this section to a social audit of the English and Welsh educational system.[13] In a sense, we have reviewed an output budget for the objective of equality of opportunity in education. The auditor's report must read: *Poor performance under present or likely future management. Share-holders need more information on their current level of returns and pattern of their distribution. Radical re-organisation of the company and its subsidiaries called for.*

APPENDIX A

The following list gives the definition and source of all the variables used in chapter 5

Rates of staying on: 16 +
Number of pupils aged sixteen years as a percentage of those aged thirteen years, three years previously
Source: Statistics of Education Vol. 1 DES (1970)

Rates of staying on: 17 +
Number of pupils aged seventeen years as a percentage of those aged thirteen years, four years previously
Source: Statistics of Education Vol. 1 DES (1970)

Secondary modern
Percentage of thirteen-year-old pupils in secondary modern schools
Source: Statistics of Education Vol. 1 DES (1970)

Comprehensive
Percentage of thirteen-year-old pupils in comprehensive schools
Source: Statistics of Education Vol. 1 DES (1970)

Grammar school 1
Percentage of pupils in all positively selective secondary schools (including direct grant and independent)
Source: Statistics of Education Vol. 1 DES (1970)

Grammar school 2
Percentage of pupils in 'traditional' grammar schools
Source: Statistics of Education Vol. 1 DES (1970)

University awards
Net uptake of fuller and lesser value awards at universities (per 1000)
Source: Statistics of Education Vol. 5 DES (1970)

Further education 1 awards
Net uptake of fuller value awards at further education establishments (per 1000)
Source: Statistics of Education Vol. 5 DES (1970)

Further education 2 awards
Net uptake of lesser value awards at further education establishments (per 1000)
Source: Statistics of Education Vol. 5 DES (1970)

Teacher training awards
College of Education students (other than postgraduates) entering courses

175

of initial teacher training (per 1000)
Source: Statistics of Education Vol. 5 DES (1970)

Pupil/teacher ratio: primary
Number of pupils per full-time teacher in primary schools
Source: Education Statistics, Institute of Municipal Treasurers and Accountants (IMTA) (1970)

Pupil/teacher ratio: secondary
Number of pupils per full-time teacher in secondary schools
Source: Education Statistics IMTA (1970)

Penny rate per pupil
Product of penny rate per pupil
Source: Education Statistics IMTA (1970)

Teachers' salaries (full-time): primary
Salaries and wages including superannuation, national insurance and other employees expenses
Source: Education Statistics IMTA (1970)

Teachers' salaries (full-time): secondary
Source: Education Statistics IMTA (1970)

Debt charges: secondary
Debt charges per secondary school pupil
Source: Education Statistics IMTA (1970)

Total expenditure: primary
Total expenditure per primary school pupil
Source: Education Statistics IMTA (1970)

Total expenditure: secondary
Total expenditure per secondary school pupil
Source: Education Statistics IMTA (1970)

Industrialisation index
Source: Rates and Rateable Values in England and Wales, Department of the Environment (DOE) and Welsh Office, HMSO (1970)

Rate call/total rateable value
Source: Rates and Rateable Values in England and Wales (DOE) and Welsh Office, HMSO (1970)

Low rateable value
Proportion of domestic hereditaments where the rateable value is less than £101
Source: Sample Census 1966 England and Wales, Housing Tables Part II, HMSO

Resources element: rate support grant
Source: Rates and Rateable Values in England and Wales (DOE) and Welsh Office, HMSO (1970)

Population size
Source: Education Statistics IMTA (1970)

Population density
Source: Education Statistics IMTA (1970)

Labour control
Proportion of the years between 1957 and 1970 during which the LEA was controlled by the Labour Party
Source: Municipal Year Books 1957–70, Municipal Journal Ltd.

High social class
Percentage of economically active and retired males in socio-economic groups (1, 2, 13) and (3 and 4)
Source: Sample Census 1966 England and Wales, Housing Table Part II, HMSO

Middle social class
Percentage of economically active and retired males in socio-economic groups (8, 9, 12, 14) and (5 and 6)
Source: Sample Census 1966 England and Wales, Housing Table Part II, HMSO

Low social class
Percentage of economically active and retired males in socio-economic groups (7, 10, 15) and (11)
Source: Sample Census 1966 England and Wales, Housing Table Part II, HMSO

Non-manual
Percentage of economically active and retired males in socio-economic groups (3 and 4), (1, 2, 13) and (5 and 6)
Source: Sample Census 1966 England and Wales, Housing Table Part II, HMSO

Manual
Percentage of economically active and retired males in socio-economic groups (8, 9, 12, 14) and (7, 10, 15) and (11)
Source: Sample Census 1966 England and Wales, Housing Table Part II, HMSO

Owner-occupiers
Proportion of households owning their own accommodation
Source: Sample Census 1966 England and Wales, Housing Tables Part II, HMSO

Council tenants
Proportion of households renting accommodation from a local authority or New Town Corporation
Source: Sample Census 1966 England and Wales, Housing Tables Part II, HMSO

Private tenants
Proportion of households renting accommodation from a private person or company
Source: Sample Census 1966 England and Wales, Housing Tables Part II, HMSO

High density
Percentage of total households at density of one person or over per room
Source: Sample Census 1966 England and Wales, Housing Tables Part II, HMSO

Amenities 1
Percentage of shared households with all amenities, i.e. hot water, fixed bath and inside w.c.
Source: Sample Census 1966 England and Wales, Housing Tables Part II, HMSO

Amenities 2
Percentage of total households with all amenities, i.e. hot water, fixed bath and inside w.c.
Source: Sample Census 1966 England and Wales, Housing Tables Part II, HMSO

APPENDIX B

Local education authorities in England and Wales fall into our six clusters in the following way:

CLUSTER 1

English County Boroughs
Barnsley, Birkenhead, Birmingham, Bootle, Burnley, Burton-on-Trent, Derby, Dewsbury, Great Yarmouth, Grimsby, Hartlepool, Leicester, Liverpool, Norwich, Nottingham, Salford, South Shields, Stoke-on-Trent, Teesside, Walsall, Warrington, Wigan, Wolverhampton, Warley

English Counties
Durham

Welsh County Boroughs
Merthyr Tydfil

Welsh Counties
Monmouthshire

Outer London Boroughs
Barking, Newham

CLUSTER 2

English County Boroughs
Bath, Bournemouth, Solihull, Southend-on-Sea, Southport

English Counties
Berkshire, Cheshire, Hertfordshire, Surrey, Sussex East. Sussex West, Yorkshire E. Riding

Outer London Boroughs
Barnet, Bexley, Bromley, Croydon, Ealing, Harrow, Hillingdon, Kingston, Redbridge, Richmond, Sutton

CLUSTER 3

English County Boroughs
Blackburn, Bradford, Carlisle, Coventry, Darlington, Doncaster, Gateshead,

179

Hull, Luton, Manchester, Newcastle-upon-Tyne, Oldham, Preston, Rochdale, Rotherham, St Helens, Sheffield, Sunderland, Tynemouth, Wakefield, Wallasey, West Bromwich

English Counties
Cumberland, Leicestershire, Oxfordshire

Welsh County Boroughs
Cardiff, Newport

Welsh Counties
Anglesey, Flintshire

CLUSTER 4

English County Boroughs
Bristol, Southampton

Outer London Boroughs
Brent, Enfield, Haringey, Hounslow, Merton, Waltham Forest

Inner London Education Authority

CLUSTER 5

English County Boroughs
Barrow, Blackpool, Bolton, Brighton, Bury, Canterbury, Chester, Dudley, Eastbourne, Exeter, Gloucester, Halifax, Hastings, Huddersfield, Ipswich, Leeds, Lincoln, Northampton, Oxford, Plymouth, Portsmouth, Reading, Stockport, Torbay, Worcester, York

English Counties
Bedfordshire, Buckinghamshire, Cambridgeshire and Ely, Cornwall, Derbyshire, Devon, Dorset, Essex, Gloucestershire, Hampshire, Hereford-shire, Huntingdonshire and Peterborough, Kent, Lancashire, Lincolnshire: Holland, Lincolnshire: Kesteven, Lincolnshire: Lindsey, Norfolk, Northamptonshire, Northumberland, Nottinghamshire, Rutland, Shropshire, Somerset, Staffordshire, Suffolk East, Suffolk West, Warwickshire, West-morland, Wiltshire, Worcestershire, Yorkshire N. Riding, Yorkshire W. Riding

Welsh County Boroughs
Swansea

Welsh Counties
Denbighshire, Glamorganshire

Outer London Boroughs
Havering

CLUSTER 6

English Counties
Isle of Wight

Welsh Counties
Breconshire, Caernarvonshire, Cardiganshire, Carmarthenshire, Merioneth,
Montgomeryshire, Pembrokeshire, Radnorshire

APPENDIX C

The following list gives the definition and source of all the variables employed in the regression models and correlations for the three cohorts. The two variable numbers distinguish the two data sets. The first number refers to the larger data set (excluding London) and the figure in brackets gives the variable number for the data set including London.

1 (1)   *Rates of staying on:* 16+ (boys)
Number of pupils aged sixteen years as a percentage of those aged thirteen years, three years previously

2 (2)   ,,   ,,   ,, (girls)
3 (3)   ,,   ,,   ,, (both)
      Source: Statistics of Education Vol. 1 DES (1970)

4 (4)   *Rates of staying on:* 17+ (boys)
Number of pupils aged seventeen years as a percentage of those aged thirteen years, four years previously

5 (5)   ,,   ,,   ,, (girls)
6 (6)   ,,   ,,   ,, (both)
      Source: Statistics of Education Vol. 1 DES (1970)

(7)   *Secondary modern*
Percentage of thirteen-year-old pupils in secondary modern schools   (boys)

(8)   ,,   ,,   ,, (girls)
7 (9)   ,,   ,,   ,, (both)
      Source: Statistics of Education Vol. 2 DES (1970)

(10)   *Comprehensive*
Percentage of thirteen-year-old pupils in comprehensive schools
                                  (boys)

(11)   ,,   ,,   ,, (girls)
8 (12)   ,,   ,,   ,, (both)
      Source: Statistics of Education Vol. 1 DES (1970)

(13)   *Grammar school 1*
Percentage of thirteen-year-old pupils in all positively selective secondary schools (grammar, technical grammar, direct grant, independent and others)   (boys)

(14)   ,,   ,,   ,, (girls)
9[1] (15)   ,,   ,,   ,, (both)
      Source: Statistics of Education Vol. 1 DES (1970)

(16)   *Grammar school 2*
Percentage of thirteen-year-old pupils in 'traditional' grammar schools (grammar and direct-grant grammar) (boys)

(17)   ,,   ,,   ,, (girls)

10 (18)   ,,   ,,   ,, (both)
         Source: Statistics of Education Vol. 1 DES (1970)

11 (19) *University awards*
         Net uptake of fuller and lesser value awards at universities (per 1000)
         Source: Statistics of Education Vol. 5 DES (1970)

12 (20) *Further education 1 awards*
         Net uptake of fuller value awards at further education establishments (per 1000)
         Source: Statistics of Education Vol. 5 DES (1970)

13 (21) *Further education 2 awards*
         Net uptake of lesser value awards at further education establishments (per 1000)
         Source: Statistics of Education Vol. 5 DES (1970)

14 (22) *Teacher training awards*
         College of Education students (other than postgraduates) entering courses of initial teacher training (per 1000)
         Source: Statistics of Education Vol. 5 DES (1970)

   (23) *Pupil/teacher ratio: primary*
         Number of pupils per full-time teacher in primary schools
         Source: Education Statistics IMTA (1970)

   (24) *Pupil/teacher ratio: secondary*
         Number of pupils per full-time teacher in secondary schools
         Source: Education Statistics IMTA (1970)

15 (25) *Penny rate per pupil*
         Product of penny rate per pupil
         Source: Education Statistics IMTA (1970)

16 (26) *Industrialisation index*
         Source: Rates and Rateable Values in England and Wales, DOE and Welsh Office, HMSO (1970)

17 (27) *Rate call/total rateable value*
         Source: Rates and Rateable Values in England and Wales, DOE and Welsh Office, HMSO (1970)

18 (28) *Low rateable value*
         Proportion of domestic hereditaments where the rateable value is less than £101
         Source: Sample Census 1966 England and Wales, Housing Tables Part II, HMSO

19 (29) *Resources element: rate support grant*
         Source: Rates and Rateable Values in England and Wales, DOE and Welsh Office, HMSO (1970)

20 (30) *Population size*
Source: Education Statistics IMTA (1970)

21 (31) *Population density*
Source: Education Statistics IMTA (1970)

22 (32) *Labour control*
Proportion of the years between 1957 and 1970 during which the LEA was controlled by the Labour Party
Source: Municipal Year Books 1957–70, Municipal Journal Ltd.

23 *Proportion of twenty-five-year-olds and over leaving school at the age of fifteen years or under (male)* (1961: *population educational experience 1*)
Source: Census 1961 England and Wales, HMSO

24 *Proportion of twenty-five-year-olds and over leaving school at the age of fifteen years or under (female)* (1961: *population educational experience 2*)
Source: Census 1961 England and Wales, HMSO

25 (33) *High social class*
Percentage of economically active and retired males in socio-economic groups (1, 2, 13) and (3 and 4)
Source: Sample Census 1966 England and Wales, Housing Tables Part II, HMSO

26 (34) *Middle social class*
Percentage of economically active and retired males in socio-economic groups (8, 9, 12, 14) and (5 and 6)
Source: Sample Census 1966 England and Wales, Housing Tables Part II, HMSO

27 (35) *Low social class*
Percentage of economically active and retired males in socio-economic groups (7, 10, 15) and (11)
Source: Sample Census 1966 England and Wales, Housing Tables Part II, HMSO

28 (36) *Non-manual*
Percentage of economically active and retired males in socio-economic groups (3 and 4), (1, 2, 13) and (5 and 6)
Source: Sample Census 1966 England and Wales, Housing Tables Part II, HMSO

29 (37) *Manual*
Percentage of economically active and retired males in socio-economic groups (8, 9, 12, 14), (7, 10, 15) and (11)
Source: Sample Census 1966 England and Wales, Housing Tables Part II, HMSO

30 (38) *Owner-occupiers*
Proportion of households owning their own accommodation

Source: Sample Census 1966 England and Wales, Housing Tables Part II, HMSO

31 (39) *Council tenants*
Proportion of households renting accommodation from a local authority or New Town Corporation
Source: Sample Census 1966 England and Wales, Housing Tables Part II, HMSO

32 (40) *Private tenants*
Proportion of households renting accommodation from a private person or company
Source: Sample Census 1966 England and Wales, Housing Tables Part II, HMSO

33 (41) *High density*
Percentage of total households at density of one person or over per room
Source: Sample Census 1966 England and Wales, Housing Tables Part II, HMSO

34 (42) *Amenities 1*
Percentage of shared households with all amenities, i.e. hot water, fixed bath and inside w.c.
Source: Sample Census 1966 England and Wales, Housing Tables Part II, HMSO

35 (43) *Amenities 2*
Percentage of total households with all amenities, i.e. hot water, fixed bath and inside w.c.
Source: Sample Census 1966 England and Wales, Housing Tables Part II, HMSO

SIXTEEN-YEAR-OLD COHORT

36 (44) *Secondary modern*
Percentage of thirteen-year-old pupils in secondary modern schools   (boys)
37 (45)   ,,   ,,   ,, (girls)
38 (46)   ,,   ,,   ,, (both)
Source: Statistics of Education Vol. 1 DES (1967)

39 (47) *Comprehensive*
Percentage of thirteen-year-old pupils in comprehensive schools
                                                              (boys)
40 (48)   ,,   ,,   ,, (girls)
41 (49)   ,,   ,,   ,, (both)
Source: Statistics of Education Vol. 1 DES (1967)

42 (50) *Grammar school 1*
Percentage of thirteen-year-old pupils in all positively selective

secondary schools   (boys)
43 (51)   ,,   ,,   ,, (girls)
44 (52)   ,,   ,,   ,, (both)
   Source: Statistics of Education Vol. 1 DES (1967)

45 (53) *Grammar school 2*
         Percentage of thirteen-year-old pupils in 'traditional' grammar
         schools   (boys)
46 (54)   ,,   ,,   ,, (girls)
47 (55)   ,,   ,,   ,, (both)
   Source: Statistics of Education Vol. 1 DES (1967)

48 (56) *Pupil/teacher ratio: primary*
         Number of pupils per full-time teacher 1959–65 (averaged)
         Source: Education Statistics IMTA (1959–65)

49 (57) *Total expenditure: primary*
         Total expenditure per primary school pupil 1959–65 (averaged)
         Source: Education Statistics IMTA (1959–65)

50 (58) *Teachers' salaries: primary*
         Salaries and wages including superannuation, national
         insurance and other employees expenses 1959–65 (averaged)
         Source: Education Statistics IMTA (1959–65)

51 (59) *Debt charges: primary*
         Debt charges per primary school pupil 1959–65 (averaged)
         Source: Education Statistics IMTA (1959–65)

52   *Pupil/teacher ratio: secondary* (1966–9 averaged)
         Source: Education Statistics IMTA (1966–9)

53   *Total expenditure: secondary* (1966–9 averaged)
         Source: Education Statistics IMTA (1966–9)

54   *Teachers' salaries: secondary* (1966–9 averaged)
         Source: Education Statistics IMTA (1966–9)

55   *Debt charges: secondary* (1966–9 averaged)
         Source: Education Statistics IMTA (1966–9)

56   *Overcrowding 1: primary*
         Proportion of classes with thirty or more pupils
         Source: DES unpublished statistics (1959–65 averaged)

57   *Overcrowding 2: primary*
         Proportion of classes with forty or more pupils
         Source: DES unpublished statistics (1959–65 averaged)

58 (60) *Overcrowding 1: secondary*
         Proportion of classes with twenty or more pupils
         Source: DES unpublished statistics (1966–9 averaged)

59 (61)   *Overcrowding 2: secondary*
           Proportion of classes with thirty or more pupils
           Source: DES unpublished statistics (1966–9 averaged)

SEVENTEEN-YEAR-OLD COHORT

60 (62)   *Secondary modern* (boys)

61 (63)   *Secondary modern* (girls)

62 (64)   *Secondary modern* (both)
           Source: Statistics of Education Vol. 1 DES (1966)

63 (65)   *Comprehensive* (boys)

64 (66)   *Comprehensive* (girls)

65 (67)   *Comprehensive* (both)
           Source: Statistics of Education Vol. 1 DES (1966)

66 (68)   *Grammar school 1* (boys)

67 (69)   *Grammar school 1* (girls)

68 (70)   *Grammar school 1* (both)
           Source: Statistics of Education Vol. 1 DES (1966)

69 (71)   *Grammar school 2* (boys)

70 (72)   *Grammar school 2* (girls)

71 (73)   *Grammar school 2* (both)
           Source: Statistics of Education Vol. 1 DES (1966)

72   *Pupil/teacher ratio: primary* (1958–64 averaged)
           Source: Education Statistics IMTA (1958–64)

73   *Total expenditure: primary* (1958–64 averaged)
           Source: Education Statistics IMTA (1958–64)

74   *Teachers' salaries: primary* (1958–64 averaged)
           Source: Education Statistics IMTA (1958–64)

75   *Debt charges: primary* (1958–64 averaged)
           Source: Education Statistics IMTA (1958–64)

76 (74)   *Pupil/teacher ratio: secondary* (1965–9 averaged)
           Source: Education Statistics IMTA (1965–9)

77 (75)   *Total expenditure: secondary* (1965–9 averaged)
           Source: Education Statistics IMTA (1965–9)

78 (76)   *Teachers' salaries: secondary* (1965–9 averaged)
            Source: Education Statistics IMTA (1965–9)

79 (77)   *Debt charges: secondary* (1965–9 averaged)
            Source: Education Statistics IMTA (1965–9)

80 (78)   *Rates of staying on:* 16+ (1969)   (boys)

81 (79)   *Rates of staying on:* 16+ (1969)   (girls)

82 (80)   *Rates of staying on:* 16+ (1969)   (both)
            Source: Statistics of Education Vol. 1 DES (1969)

83   *Overcrowding 1: primary* (1958–64 averaged)
            Proportion of classes with thirty pupils or more
            Source: DES unpublished statistics (1958–64)

84   *Overcrowding 2: primary* (1958–64 averaged)
            Proportion of classes with forty pupils or more
            Source: DES unpublished statistics (1958–64)

85 (81)   *Overcrowding 1: secondary* (1965–9 averaged)
            Proportion of classes with twenty pupils or more
            Source: DES unpublished statistics (1965–9)

86 (82)   *Overcrowding 2: secondary* (1965–9 averaged)
            Proportion of classes with thirty pupils or more
            Source: DES unpublished statistics (1965–9)

NINETEEN-YEAR-OLD COHORT

87   *Overcrowding 1: primary* (1956–62 averaged)
            Proportion of classes with thirty pupils or more
            Source: DES unpublished statistics (1956–62)

88   *Overcrowding 2: primary* (1956–62 averaged)
            Proportion of classes with forty pupils or more
            Source: DES unpublished statistics (1956–62)

89   *Overcrowding 1: secondary* (1963–9 averaged)
            Proportion of classes with twenty pupils or more
            Source: DES unpublished statistics (1963–9)

90   *Overcrowding 2: secondary* (1963–9 averaged)
            Proportion of classes with thirty pupils or more
            Source: DES unpublished statistics (1963–9)

91   *Percentage graduates*
            Percentage of teachers in each LEA who are graduates (1964)
                                                        (men)
92   ,,   ,,   ,, (women)
93   ,,   ,,   ,, (both)
            Source: DES unpublished statistics (1964)

94   Percentage of teachers in each LEA who are graduates (1967)
                                                           (men)
95   ,,   ,,   ,,   (women)
96   ,,   ,,   ,,   (both)
          Source: DES unpublished statistics (1967)

97   Percentage of teachers in each LEA who are graduates (1970)
                                                           (men)
98   ,,   ,,   ,,   (women)
99[2]   ,,   ,,   ,,   (both)
          Source: DES unpublished statistics (1970)

100   *Secondary modern*   (boys)

101   *Secondary modern*   (girls)

102   *Secondary modern*   (both)
          Source: Statistics of Education Vol. 1 DES (1964)

103   *Comprehensive*   (boys)

104   *Comprehensive*   (girls)

105   *Comprehensive*   (both)
          Source: Statistics of Education Vol. 1 DES (1964)

106   *Grammar school 1*   (boys)

107   *Grammar school 1*   (girls)

108   *Grammar school 1*   (both)
          Source: Statistics of Education Vol. 1 DES (1964)

109   *Grammar school 2*   (boys)

110   *Grammar school 2*   (girls)

111   *Grammar school 2*   (both)
          Source: Statistics of Education Vol. 1 DES (1964)

112   *Pupil/teacher ratio: primary* (1956–62 averaged)
          Source: Education Statistics IMTA (1956–62)

113   *Total expenditure: primary* (1956–62 averaged)
          Source: Education Statistics IMTA (1956–62)

114   *Teachers' salaries: primary* (1956–62 averaged)
          Source: Education Statistics IMTA (1956–62)

115   *Debt charges: primary* (1956–62 averaged)
          Source: Education Statistics IMTA (1956–62)

116   *Pupil/teacher ratio: secondary* (1963–9 averaged)
       Source: Education Statistics IMTA (1963–9)

117   *Total expenditure: secondary* (1963–9 averaged)
       Source: Education Statistics IMTA (1963–9)

118   *Teachers' salaries: secondary* (1963–9 averaged)
       Source: Education Statistics IMTA (1963–9)

119   *Debt charges: secondary* (1963–9 averaged)
       Source: Education Statistics IMTA (1963–9)

120   *Rates of staying on:* 16+   (boys)

121   *Rates of staying on:* 16+   (girls)

122   *Rates of staying on:* 16+   (both)
       Source: Statistics of Education Vol. 1 DES (1967)

123   *Rates of staying on:* 17+   (boys)

124   *Rates of staying on:* 17+   (girls)

125   *Rates of staying on:* 17+   (both)
       Source: Statistics of Education Vol. 1 DES (1968)

NOTES

INTRODUCTION

1 N. Boaden *Urban Policy Making* London, Cambridge University Press (1971)
2 G. Taylor and N. Ayres *Born and Bred Unequal* London, Longmans (1969)
3 J. Eggleston 'Some Environmental Correlates of Extended Secondary Education in England' in D. F. Swift (ed.) *Basic Readings in the Sociology of Education* London, Routledge and Kegan Paul (1969)
4 Northern Economic Planning Council 'Challenge of the Changing North – Education: Part I' Newcastle (1970)
5 D. S. Byrne and W. Williamson 'The Myth of the Restricted Code' University of Durham Working Paper in Sociology No. 1 (1971)
6 D. S. Byrne and W. Williamson 'Some Intraregional Variations in Educational Provision and their Bearing upon Educational Attainment: The Case of the North-east' *Sociology* 6, 1 (January 1971)
7 *ibid.*, p. 71
8 D. S. Byrne and W. Williamson *op. cit.* (1971)
9 *ibid.*, p. 6

1   THE PROBLEM STATED

1 R. H. Tawney *Equality* London, Allen and Unwin (1931) quoted from H. Silver *Equal Opportunity in Education* London, Methuen (1973) p. 51
2 A. H. Halsey *Educational Priority* London, HMSO (1972) p. 7
3 *ibid.*, p. 8
4 Tawney *op. cit.* p. 52
5 Halsey *op. cit.*
6 C. Jencks *et al. Inequality* London, Basic Books (1972) p. 52
7 *ibid.*, p. 255
8 *ibid.*, p. 255
9 J. W. B. Douglas 'A Blunt Instrument' *New Society* 25, 572 (1973)
10 Central Advisory Council for Education (England) *Children and Their Primary Schools: A Report* (Plowden Report) 2 vols. London, HMSO (1967)
11 G. Taylor and N. Ayres *Born and Bred Unequal* London, Longmans (1969)
12 See, for example, N. Boaden *Urban Policy Making* London, Cambridge University Press (1971); D. S. Byrne and W. Williamson 'The Myth of the Restricted Code' University of Durham Working Paper in Sociology No. 1 (1971)
13 Central Advisory Council for Education (England) *15–18* (Newsom Report) 2 vols. London, HMSO (1963)

14 Plowden Report (1967)
15 See, for example, B. Jackson *Streaming: An Educational System in Miniature* London, Routledge and Kegan Paul (1964). D. H. Hargreaves *Social Relations in a Secondary School* London, Routledge and Kegan Paul (1967)
16 National Children's Bureau *From Birth to Seven* London, Longmans (1972)
17 B. R. Clarke 'The Cooling-out Function in Higher Education' in A. H. Halsey, J. Floud and C. A. Anderson (eds.) *Education, Economy and Society* New York, The Free Press of Glencoe (1961) p. 513

2 MODELS OF ATTAINMENT

1 D. C. Morton and D. R. Watson 'Compensatory Education and Contemporary Liberalism in the United States: A Sociological Review' *International Review of Education* XVII 3 (1971)
2 *ibid.*, p. 292
3 M. Kogan *The Politics of Education* Harmondsworth, Middlesex, Penguin (1971) p. 91
4 *ibid.*, p. 185
5 Committee on Higher Education (England) *Higher Education* (Robbins Report) London, HMSO (1963) p. 7 para 28
6 Central Advisory Council for Education (England) *Half our Future: A Report* (Newsom Report) London, HMSO (1963) p. 6 paras. 15 and 18
7 F. Riessman *The Culturally Deprived Child* New York, Harper and Row (1962)
8 N. Friedman 'Cultural Deprivation: a Commentary in the Sociology of Knowledge' *Journal of Educational Thought* 1, 2 (1967) p. 91
9 D. C. McClelland *The Achievement Motive* New York, Appleton (1953)
10 J. A. Kahl ' "Common Man" Boys' in A. H. Halsey, J. Floud and C. A. Anderson (eds.) *Education, Economy and Society* New York, The Free Press of Glencoe (1961)
11 D. P. Moynihan *The Negro Family: The Case for National Action* Cambridge, Mass. MIT Press (1967)
12 B. Bernstein 'A Critique of the Concept of Compensatory Education' *Class Codes and Control* vol. 1 London, Paladin (1973), p. 215
13 *ibid.*, p. 216
14 Mario D. Fantini and G. Weinstein *The Disadvantaged: Challenge to Education* New York, Harper and Row (1968)
15 J. Holt *How Children Fail* London, Pelican (1969)
16 E. Reimer *School is Dead* Harmondsworth, Middlesex, Penguin (1971)
17 H. Kohl *36 Children* London, Victor Gollanz (1968)
18 Central Advisory Council for Education (England) *Children and Their Primary Schools: A Report* (Plowden Report) London, HMSO (1967) para 136
19 H. Glennerster 'The Plowden Research' *Journal of the Royal Statistical Society* Series A, 132, 2 (1969)
20 Plowden Report, p. 28
21 B. Bernstein and B. Davies 'Some Sociological Comments on Plowden'

in R. Peters *Perspectives on Plowden* London, Routledge and Kegan Paul (1969)

22 A. H. Halsey 'Education and Social Class in 1972' in K. Jones (ed.) *Yearbook of Social Policy* London, Routledge and Kegan Paul (forthcoming)

23 B. Simon *Intelligence, Psychology and Education: a Marxist Critique* London, Lawrence and Wishart (1971)

24 J. Ford *Social Class and the Comprehensive School* London, Routledge and Kegan Paul (1970)

25 B. Jackson *Streaming: An Educational System in Miniature* London, Routledge and Kegan Paul (1964)

26 Joan Barker-Lunn *Streaming in the Primary Schools* Slough, NFER (1970)

27 D. Hargreaves *Social Relations in a Secondary Modern School* London, Routledge and Kegan Paul (1967)

28 W. Williamson and D. S. Byrne 'Research, Theory and Policy in Education: Some Notes on a Self-sustaining System' *Education, Economy and Politics: Case Studies Parts 1 and 2* Course E352, Bletchley, The Open University (1973)

29 D. Lawton *Social Class, Language and Education* London, Routledge and Kegan Paul (1968)

30 H. Rosen *Language and Class* Bristol, Falling Wall Press (1972)

31 K. Coates and R. Silburn *Poverty: The Forgotten Englishmen* Harmondsworth, Middlesex, Penguin (1970)

32 C. A. Valentine *Culture and Poverty* Chicago, Chicago University Press (1969)

33 Moynihan *op cit.*

34 C. B. Cox and A. E. Dyson *The Black Papers on Education* London, Davis-Poynter Ltd (1971)

35 Morton and Watson *op cit.*

3 A SOCIO-SPATIAL MODEL OF EDUCATIONAL ATTAINMENT

1 A. H. Halsey 'Education and Social Class in 1972' in K. Jones (ed.) *Yearbook of Social Policy 1973* London, Routledge and Kegan Paul (forthcoming)

2 *ibid.*

3 *ibid.*

4 M. Weber 'Class, Status, Party' in H. H. Gerth and C. Wright Mills *From Max Weber* London, Routledge and Kegan Paul (1970) pp. 180–94. Max Weber puts it this way:

In our terminology, 'classes' are not communities; they merely represent possible, and frequent, bases for communal action. We may speak of a 'class' when (1) a number of people have in common a specific causal component of their life chances, in so far as (2) this component is represented exclusively by economic interests in the possession of goods and opportunities for income. and (3) is represented under the conditions of the commodity or labor markets.

5 G. Taylor and N. Ayres *Born and Bred Unequal* London, Longmans (1969)

6   B. Davies *Social Needs and Resources in Local Services* London, Michael Joseph (1968)
7   F. Engels *The Condition of the Working Class in England in 1844,* first published 1845, first published in English in 1892
8   R. Pahl 'Poverty and the Urban System' in M. Chisholm and G. Manners *Spatial Policy Problems of the British Economy* London, Cambridge University Press (1971) p. 130
9   Central Advisory Council for Education (England) *Half Our Future: A Report* (Newsom Report) London, HMSO (1963)
10 Central Advisory Council for Education (England) *Children and Their Primary Schools* (Plowden Report) London, HMSO (1967)
11 Pahl *op cit.* p. 134
12 D. Harvey *Social Justice in the City* London, Michael Joseph (1973) p. 23
13 Taylor and Ayres *op cit.*
14 J. Rex 'The Sociology of a Zone of Transition' in R. E. Pahl (ed.) *Readings in Urban Sociology* London, Pergamon (1968)
15 *ibid.,* p. 215
16 R. Pahl *Whose City?* London, Longmans (1970) p. 215
17 *ibid.,* pp. 215–16
18 M. Blang *An Introduction to the Economics of Education* London, Allen Lane (1970) especially chapter 2
19 E. F. Dennison 'Proportion of Income Differentials Among Education Groups due to Additional Education' in J. Vaizey (ed.) *The Residual Factor and Economic Growth* Paris, OECD (1964)
20 R. K. Kelsall *et al. Graduates: The Sociology of an Elite* London, Methuen (1972)
21 C. Jencks *et al. Inequality* London, Allen Lane (1972)
22 J. W. B. Douglas 'A Blunt Instrument' *New Society* 25, 572 (1973)
23 J. H. Goldthorpe and D. Lockwood 'Affluence and the British Class Structure' *Sociological Review* 11 (1963)
24 B. Abel-Smith and P. Townsend *The Poor and The Poorest* London, Occasional Papers in Social Administration No. 17 (1965)
25 A. Westoby and G. Williams 'How Much is Your Degree Worth?' *Where* (March 1973)
26 J. E. Meade *Efficiency, Equality and the Ownership of Property* London, Allen and Unwin (1964)
27 A. B. Atkinson *Poverty in Britain and the Reform of Social Security* University of Cambridge, Department of Applied Economics Occasional Paper 18 (1969)
28 D. Wedderburn and C. Craig 'Relative Deprivation in Work'. Paper presented to the British Association for the Advancement of Science, Exeter (1969)
29 Central Advisory Council for Education (England) *15–18* (Crowther Report) London, HMSO (1959)
30 N. Dennis *Public Participation and Planners' Blight* London, Faber and Faber (1972)
31 N. Dennis *People and Planning* London, Faber and Faber (1970)
32 J. G. Davies *The Evangelistic Bureaucrat* London, Tavistock (1972)
33 *ibid.,* p. 2
34 E. Midwinter *Priority Education* Harmondsworth, Middlesex, Penguin (1972)
35 R. H. Tawney *Equality* London, Allen and Unwin (1931)

4 MEASURES FOR MODELS

1 The term 'socially significant educational attainment' refers to rates of staying on at school beyond the statutory minimum leaving age, and the uptake of local authority awards for higher education. It does not refer to cognitive abilities. The assumption behind the use of this measure is that children who stay on at school are more likely than those who do not to enter non-manual employment. Staying on at school is, therefore, the first step on the escalator to social mobility. It is for this reason that we regard such attainment as socially significant.

2 See, for example, N. M. Blalock *Causal Inferences in Non-experimental Research* Chapel Mill, University of North Carolina Press (1961)

3 S. Bowles and H. M. Levin 'The Determinants of Scholastic Achievement – an Appraisal of Some Recent Evidence' *Journal of Human Resources* III, 1 (Winter 1968) pp. 8–9

4 J. L. Hammond 'Two Sources of Error in Ecological Correlations' *American Sociological Review* Vol. 38, No. 6 (December 1973) p. 773

5 This was derived from the 1961 Census and was, therefore, unavailable for the Outer London Boroughs which were created subsequent to that Census. We excluded all the Greater London area, including Inner London, for which the data were available. This tends to balance the necessary omission of Outer London. There have been boundary changes affecting other LEAs between 1961 and 1970 (our base year). Where these were gross we tried to allow for them, e.g. where new LEAs were created from existing local authority areas. However, the effect of boundary changes is in general bound to be conservative, i.e. tending to reduce calculated relationships. The problem is not, therefore, a major one.

6 G. Taylor and N. Ayres *Born and Bred Unequal* London, Longmans (1969)

7 Calculated as described in Appendix C, p. 181. This seemed to us to be an indication of willingness to spend ratepayers' money, and can be regarded, therefore, as in indication of radical policy. It is also an indication of wealth, as the wealthier authorities, who are well above 'standard product' of a penny rate, do not need to call in so much of their potential income.

8 These were obtained from DES records (see Appendix C, pp. 186–7)

9 J. Eggleston 'Some Environmental Correlates of Extended Secondary Education in England' in D. F. Swift (ed.) *Basic Readings in the Sociology of Education* London, Routledge and Kegan Paul (1969)

10 At the time our data set was prepared this was the most recent year for which 'attainment' data were available.

11 Those excluded were Teesside, Torbay and Warley.

12 Due to the creation of new Outer London Boroughs in the early sixties.

13 Primarily because data relating to environmental factors, and all the socio-economic data, were derived from the 1966 Sample Census. Again we would argue that the effect of changes is to diminish the strength of relationships and, therefore, this results in a conservative bias.

14 That is to say that two things may 'cause' each other simultaneously.

To some degree this is true of educational provision since the rate of staying on beyond sixteen years of age was an important determinant in the needs element of rate support grant, and hence of provision.

15 Especially of path analysis. A mathematical solution to the problem exists. See Van de Geer *Introduction to multivariate analysis for the social sciences* San Francisco, Freeman (1971)

16 A. Rivlin *Systematic Thinking for Social Action* Washington, Brookings (1971). We dislike the positivistic details of the term. We regard quantitative data as merely one form of general historical data concerned with the historical existence of relationships rather than 'scientific' validity.

17 Using the Clustan: 1A programme package.

18 T. N. Clark 'Urban typologies and political outputs' *Social Science Information* 9, 6, p. 7 (1971)

19 LEAS change control. This was very much the case in the late 1960s and had marked effects on gross policies especially with regard to form of comprehensive secondary education. However education 'policy' has a lot of momentum in that previous commitments govern current actions; thus even here stability is the norm, at least in the medium term.

20 K. C. Land 'Principles of Path Analysis' in E. F. Borgatta (ed.) *Sociological Methodology* San Francisco, Jossey-Bass (1969) pp. 3–4

21 'Debt charges per pupil' is as much a function of the time at which loans were raised as anything else. If debt charges are high, this indicates that an extensive building programme has been undertaken in recent years. However, many 'high-class' LEAS inherited a stock of good physical capital from the inter-war years, the current costs of which would be negligible.

22 Central Advisory Council for Education (England) *Half Our Future: A Report* (Newsom Report) London, HMSO (1963)

23 R. E. Pahl 'Spatial Structure and Social Structure' *Whose City?* London, Longman (1970) p. 187

24 R. D. Gastil 'The Relationship of Regional Cultures to Educational Performance' *Sociology of Education* 45, 4 (1972) pp. 408–25

25 de Geer *op cit.*, p. 113

26 O. D. Duncan 'Path Analysis: Some Sociological Examples' *American Journal of Sociology* 72, 1 (July 1966) pp. 1–16; Land *op cit.*; D. R. Heise 'Some Problems of Path Analysis' in E. F. Borgatta (ed.) *Sociological Methodology* San Francisco, Jossey-Bass (1969)

27 Land *op cit.* p. 9. However, K. Hope in 'Path Analysis: Supplementary Procedures' *Sociology* 5 (1971) has said: 'A path coefficient cannot, in a straightforward sense, be regarded as yielding the square root of the proportion of the variance of a posterior variable explained by an anterior variable.' Having regard to Hope's strictures it seems to us that the use of partial correlation procedures ought to be paramount.

28 Bowles and Levin *op cit.* discuss this issue in a relevant context (pp. 14–16) and in their subsequent reply to Coleman's rejoinder 'More on Multi-Collinearity and the Effectiveness of Schools' *Journal of Human Resources* 3 (Summer 1968)

29 J. S. Coleman 'The Concept of Equality of Educational Opportunity' *Harvard Educational Review* 38 (Winter 1968), p. 8

5 TYPES OF LOCAL AUTHORITY

1 G. Orwell *The Road to Wigan Pier* London, Penguin (1962) p. 46
2 *ibid.,* p. 19
3 D. M. Clark *Greater Manchester Votes* Manchester, Redrose Publications (1973)
4 Clark *op cit.*
5 Clark *op cit.*
6 D. Read *Edwardian England. 1901–15 Society and Politics* London, Harrap (1972)
7 The Deeplish Study *Improvement possibilities in a district of Rochdale* London, HMSO (1966) p. 5
8 Open University Broadcast 'Politics, Authority and Attainment' Course E.352 (Education, Economy and Politics)
9 P. J. Madgwick, N. Griffiths and V. Walker *The Politics of Rural Wales: A Study of Cardiganshire* London, Hutchinson and Co. Ltd. (1973)
10 Madgwick *et al. op cit.*
11 Madgwick *et al. op cit.*
12 E. J. Hobsbawm *Industry and Empire* Harmondsworth, Middlesex, Penguin (1969)
13 National Children's Bureau *From Birth to Seven* London, Longmans (1972)
14 Central Advisory Council for Education *Primary Education in Wales* (Gittins Report) London, HMSO (1968)
15 Madgwick *et al. op cit.*

8 THE NINETEEN-PLUS COHORT

1 D. S. Byrne and W. Williamson 'Some Intraregional Variations in Educational Provision and their Bearing on Educational Attainment: The Case of the North East' *Sociology* 6, 1 (January 1971)
2 R. K. Kelsall, A. Poole and A. Kuhn *Graduates: The Sociology of an Elite* London, Methuen and Co. Ltd. (1972)

9 CLASS, PROVISION AND EDUCATIONAL ATTAINMENT

1 J. S. Coleman *Equality of Educational Opportunity* US Office of Education, Washington (1966)
2 C. Jencks *et al. Inequality* London, Allen Lane (1973)
3 It is extremely difficult to relate system provision, as it cannot be defined at a level less than school class, and then with considerable difficulty to individuals. Attempts to do so have typically, and correctly, been accused of committing an 'ecological fallacy'.
4 J. W. B. Douglas 'A Blunt Instrument' *New Society* 25, 572 (1973)
5 R. Pahl *Whose City?* London, Longmans (1973)
6 J. Rex 'The Sociology of a Zone of Transition' in R. E. Pahl (ed.) *Readings in Urban Sociology* London, Pergamon (1968)

7   This issue bears further elaboration at this point. We can readily contend, following Pahl and Rex, that the spatial and administrative constraints which congrue and operate so tightly in the state educational system in England and Wales define 'educational classes' in the way that housing allocation procedures define housing classes in relation to local authority housing stock. This implies that 'educational class' relates to a non-economic hierarchy. Contemporary Weberians have devoted considerable attention to this particular perspective, especially in relation to the operation of bureaucratically modulated allocations in contrast to market system allocations. An important component of this body of thinking has been a concern with the specifically spatial constraints, a concern best exemplified by David Harvey's liberal formulations. The socialist alternatives, as Harvey clearly recognises, involve the congruence of other inequalities with basal inequality stemming from the organisation of productive processes. We will leave until the next chapter a more detailed discussion both of this issue and of the closely related problem of how far 'educational classes' can acquire a class consciousness; become classes for themselves as well as classes in themselves.

8   D. Swift, B. Williamson and D. Byrne *Education, Economy and Politics: Case Studies, Parts 1 and 2* Bletchley, The Open University Press (1973)

9   'Debt charges per pupil' are largely a function of how recently money has been borrowed, and are no real index of the quality of the physical fabric of schools. If debt charges are high, it is likely that an authority has undertaken an extensive building programme. However, an authority with low debt charges may have a legacy of good pre-war grammar schools, whose current capital cost has been rendered negligible by inflation.

10   Central Advisory Council for Education (England) *Half Our Future* (Newsom Report) London, HMSO (1963)

11   Central Advisory Council for Education (England) *Children and their Primary Schools* (Plowden Report) London, HMSO (1967)

12   The method of assessment of needs element of rate support grant in operation when our data were collected was very heavily conditioned by rates of staying on at school in different local authorities. Recent developments have not substantially altered this bias.

13   C. A. Valentine *Culture and Poverty: Critique and Counter Proposals* University of Chicago Press (1968)

14   We should note that 'general environmental conditions' is likely to be the only index of educational built environment available, and this may incorporate a dimension of specifically educational inequality.

15   The model represented by Fig. 9.2 is a component of the model represented by Fig. 9.4

16   Coleman *op cit.*

17   G. Hodgson 'Inequality: Do Schools Make a Difference?' reprinted in H. Silver (ed.) *Equal Opportunity in Education* Methuen (1973) p. 356

10   CONCLUSION: SOCIAL POLICY, IDEOLOGY AND EDUCATIONAL ATTAINMENT

1   R. M. Titmuss *Income Distribution and Social Change* London, Allen and Unwin (1962) p. 34
2   D. Harvey (quoting from Titmuss *op. cit.*) *Social Justice and the City* London, Arnold (1973) p. 53
3   M. J. Bowman 'The Human Investment Revolution in Economic Thought' *Sociology of Education* 39 (1966) p. 113
4   C. Jencks *et al. Inequality* London, Allen Lane (1973)
5   J. S. Coleman 'The Concept of Equality of Educational Opportunity' *Harvard Educational Review* 38, 1 (Winter 1968) pp. 7–22
6   T. Husén *Social Background and Educational Career* Paris, OECD (1972) p. 36
7   Coleman *op cit.*
8   See, for example, B. Simon *Education and the Labour Movement 1870–1920* Studies in the History of Education Vol. 2, London, Lawrence and Wishart (1965); and D. Rubinstein and B. Simon *The Evolution of the Comprehensive School 1926–66* London, Routledge and Kegan Paul (1969)
9   M. Segré, L. Tanguy and M–F Lortic 'A New Ideology of Education' *Social Forces* 50, 3 (March 1972) p. 313
10 Husén, *op. cit.*
11 Plowden Report quoted by W. Van der Eyken *Education, The Child and Society,* Harmondsworth, Penguin (1973) p. 489
12 der Eyken *op. cit.* p. 489
13 See Educational Planning Paper No. 1, London, DES (1970)

APPENDIX C

1   As the SPSS Pearson Correlation programme which we employed has a maximum input of 125 variables, we simply employed 'total' in different school types at thirteen years.

2   In the regression models for the sixteen-year-old and seventeen-year-old cohorts we employed variable 99 (i.e. percentage total graduates 1970). In the nineteen-plus cohort regression models we used variable 96 (percentage total graduates in 1967)

3   The correlation matrices for both data sets are not reproduced here for reasons of space. They are available from Department of Sociology and Social Administration, University of Durham.

4   The data employed throughout this book will be lodged with the SSRC Data Archive, University of Essex, and will be available on request from them.

5   In the regression models the following variables were employed under the following headings:

	All three cohorts	
	Excluding London	Including London
High social class ...	25	33
Middle social class ...	26	34
Low social class	27	35
Non-manual	28	36
Manual	29	37
1961: population educational experience ...	23, 24	—
All class	25–9	33–7
All class + 1961: population educational experience	23–9	—
Environmental factors ...	16, 18, 20, 21 33–5	26, 28, 30, 31, 41–3
Provision: 16 + ...	36–59, 99	44–61
Provision: 17 + ...	60–79, 83–6, 99	62–77, 81, 82
Provision: 19 + ...	87–90, 96, 100–19	—

INDEX

This index was compiled by Pete Clarkson

Abel-Smith, B. and Townsend, P. 40
Aberfan, the disaster of 79, 81
Atkinson, A. B. 40
attainment – *see* educational attainment
attainment rates 9, 54, 71–75, 86, 95

Barker-Lunn, J. 26
Barnsley 72
Barrow-in-Furness 75
Bath 73
Belfield Community School, Rochdale 94, 95
Berkshire 72
Bernstein, B. 16, 19, 20, 23, 27
Bernstein, B. and Davies, B. 25
Bevan, Aneurin 79, 82
Blackpool 75, 102–107; attainment rates 106; educational expenditure 104–105; educational provision 103–104; further education 103–104; policy 105–106; social class background 102–103
Blalock, N. M. 48
Blaug, M. 39
Boaden, N. ix
Bootle 72
Bowles, S. and Levin, H. N. 49
Boyle, Lord 15
Breconshire 75
Bristol 74, 98–102; attainment, rates of 102; educational policy 99–101; provision 99–101; private education 99; social class background 98

Caernarvonshire 8, 75
capitalist society 4, 28; welfare capitalist societies 168
Cardiff 73
Cardiganshire 75, 107–109; attainment 108; educational policy 108; Provision 109; social class background 108
Carmarthenshire 76
causal models 48, 56, 59–66, 117–129, 136–143, 149–152
Cheshire 73
city, the (*see also* socio-spatial system) 36
Claimants' Unions 172–173
Clarke, Burton R. 10
cluster analysis 49, 53, 55–59, 68–70, 109–110; relocation method 58; Ward's method (hierarchical fusion) 57
Coates, K. and Silburn, R. 27
Cobden, Richard 92
cognitive skills 5, 9, 26
cohort xi, 48, 50
Coleman, J. S. 49, 65, 153, 166, 169, 170
community development 44
compensatory education – *see* education
Co-operative Movements, The 92
correlates, of attainment 111–115; of further and higher education 144; among provision 117, 134–136, 149; of provision 115–116, 132–134, 146–147
correlation techniques, canonical 49; multiple 63, 117; partial 63–66, 111–129
Crosland, Antony 15, 20
Crowther Report, The 40
Croydon 73
Cultural deprivation 21, 22, 24, 28
culture of poverty, the 22, 160–161

data 49; cross-sectional 54, 55–59; longitudinal 54, 59–66; 'natural experiment' 56, 60; quantitative 66
Davies, B. 33
Davies, J. 43, 44

Deeplish Study, The 93
Dennis, N. 42, 43, 44
Dennison, E. F. 39
Department of Education and Science (DES) 15, 90
Department of Sociology and Social Administration, University of Durham ix
Doncaster 73
Douglas, J. W. B. 6, 16, 19, 21, 40, 153
Duncan, O. D. 64

ecology, social 36, 38; ecological fallacy, the 50
Education Act, The (1944) 17, 18, 21
Education Act, United States of America (1965) 21
education, compensatory 5, 6, 13, 14, 15, 22, 23, 171; comprehensive system of 73, 75, 79, 81, 85, 89, 93, 99, 100, 103; elementary 17; further 99, 146; and income 38–41; investment in 39; and the labour market 3, 40, 41; positive discrimination in 4, 5, 20, 25, 26, 28, 34, 173; secondary 17, 54, 79–80, 84, 89–90, 93, 99–101, 103; and social class 1, 2, 4
educational attainment ix, 2, 3, 7, 9, 27, 46, 48, 54–55, 62, 109–110, 168, 169; correlates of 111–115, 130–132; and class background 125–129; spatial variation in 156–166
educational life-chances 1, 9, 12, 14, 33, 41, 46, 52, 97, 166
educational opportunity 39, 45, 170; equality of 1, 2, 5, 10, 16, 17, 20, 27, 65, 169–174; inequality of 3, 4, 7, 12, 32, 153–154, 169; socio-spatial 154–166
educational planning 17, 18, 20, 43, 44
educational policy 1. 4, 45, 53, 162–163, 165, 170; egalitarian 163
Educational Priority Areas (EPA) 8, 12, 16, 25
educational provision ix, 45, 53, 54, 71–75, 156; and attainment 155–166; correlates among 117,

134–136, 149; correlates of 115–116, 132–134, 146–147; and social class 159–166; resources x, 33, 34, 54
Eggleston, J. ix, 53
employment, life-chances 13
Engels, F. 33
environmental factors 52–53, 71–75, 157, 158; and social class 159
Exeter 75
externalities, economic theory of 37, 38, 42

Fantini, M. D. and Weinstein, G. 23
Floud, J. 19
Ford, J. 26
Friedman, N. 21

Gastil, R. D. 63
gatekeepers, social 38, 42, 44
Gateshead 73, 96–98; attainment 96; policy 97; provision 97; social class background 96
Gittins Report, The 109
Glennerster, H. 24
Goldthorpe, J. H. and Lockwood, D. 40

Halsey, A. H. 1, 2, 3, 4, 8, 9, 15, 16, 19, 25, 31, 32
Hammond, J. L. 50
Hargreaves, D. 26
Harvey, D. 36, 167
Heise, D. R. 64
Himmelweit, H. 19
Hobsbawm, E. J. 108
Holt, J. 23
housing, classes 36–37, 43; conditions 43, 71–75, 84; life-chances 13, 33, 36; market 36–37, 44
Husén, T. 169, 171

Income 6, 7, 29, 33–35, 37, 45, 46; definition of 167, 168; distribution of 38, 41, 42, 44, 167; and education 38–41; opportunities 39, 41; real 33–35; social 167–171
inequality (see also educational opportunity) 5, 6
intelligence tests 19

Jackson, B. 16, 26

Jencks, C. 5, 6, 7, 8, 9, 39, 40, 153, 154, 168, 169

Kahl, J. A. 22
Kelsall, R. K. 39, 146
Kogan, M. 15
Kohl, H. 23
labour market (*see also* education and the labour market) 4, 45, 46, 170; Greater London 115
Lancashire 71
Land, K. 61, 64
language codes 20, 21
language development programmes 20
Lawton, D. 27
Leeds 75
Leicestershire plan (comprehensive reorganisation) 93
liberalism 92
Liverpool Education Committee 16
local authorities, types of 71–76; Labour controlled 71, 73, 74, 84, 97; Conservative controlled 72, 74, 88, 102
Local Education Authorities (LEA's) ix, x, 46, 52, 55; expenditure 39, 45, 48, 71–75; policy 53; (*see also* individual case studies, Chapter 5)
Lowry, L. S. 71

McClelland, D. C. 22
Madgwick, P. J. et al 108, 109
Mays, J. B. 16
Meade, J. E. 40
Merioneth 76
Merthyr Tydfil 72, 78–83; attainment 82; nursery schools 80–81; policy 81–82; provision 79–81; social class background 79
Methodism 92
Mills, C. Wright 14
Montgomeryshire 76
Morton, D. C. and Watson, D. R. 13, 14
Moynihan, D. 22, 28
multiple regression analysis 49, 111–129
multi-variate analysis 48

National Children's Bureau, report of 9
'natural experiment' 56, 60

Newcastle-upon-Tyne 43, 73
Newsom Report, The 8, 16, 34, 63, 157
Northern Economic Planning Council, reports of ix
Northern Economic Planning Region ix
Norwich 72
Norwood Report, The 19
nursery schools/pre-school education – *see* schools

occupational structure 39
occupations manual 40, 51, 73, 74, 75; non-manual 40, 41, 51, 72, 74; entrance requirements 41
Orwell, George 71, 83, 84

Pahl, R. A. 34, 35, 36, 38, 39, 42, 63, 154
parent teacher association (PTA) 13, 71, 89
path analysis 64
Pembrokeshire 76
planning, physical 42, 43; 'planners' blight' 42
Plowden Report, The 7, 8, 16, 23, 25, 26, 34, 90, 94, 157, 173
policy (*see also* educational policy) ix
positive discrimination – *see* education
power and socio-spatial systems – *see* socio-spatial systems
pre-school children (*see also* nursery schools) 13
Priestley, J. B. 96
Project Headstart (U.S.A.) 21, 23
provision – *see* educational provision

Radnorshire 76
Read, D. 87
regression analysis 63
Reimer, E. 23
resources (*see also* educational provision) ix; distribution of 38
Rex, J. 36, 37, 154
Riessman, F. 21
Robbins Report, The 16
Rochdale 73, 92–96; attainment 95; policy 94–95; provision 93–95; social class background 92–93

Rosen, H. 27

schools 23; comprehensive 79, 80, 84, 85, 88, 89, 93, 97, 99, 100, 101, 103, 105; direct grant 72, 74, 88; elementary 3, 63; grammar 18, 54, 72, 74, 85, 86, 88, 99, 103, 105; nursery 81, 84, 90, 93, 101, 104; primary 80, 84, 89, 90, 93, 94, 95, 101; private 41, 48; public 4, 41, 88, 99; secondary modern 18, 72, 74, 79, 88, 99, 103; sixth-form college 85, 89, 91
Segré, M. *et al* 170
Simon, B. 26, 170
sixth-form college – *see* schools
social class (*see also* education and social class) x, 1, 7, 31, 62; class background 51–52, 71–75; and attainment 125–129, 159, 169; statistical definitions of 65; structural concept of 42
social mobility 13
social policy 171–174
Social Science Research Council ix, x, 68
social services, spatial distribution of 33, 34
social stratification 35
socio-cultural perspective 4, 160
socio-spatial systems 11, 12, 32–33, 35–38; definition of 32–33; educational 50, 51, 55, 56, 60, 62; and power 42–46; and inequality 154–166
Solihull 70, 73, 86–92; attainment 91–92; expenditure 90; policy 90–91; provision 88–90; social class background 87–88
Southampton 74
South Shields 72
Spens Report, The 17, 18, 19

streaming 26
Sunderland 73; medical officer of health, report of (1936) 43; slum clearance in 43
Surrey 73
Swift, D. F. 16

Tawney, R. H. 1, 3, 4, 33, 171
Taylor, G. and Ayres, N. ix, 8, 33, 36, 52
teacher training (*see also* attainment, attainment rates and case studies, Chapter 5) 152; correlates of 146
territorial justice 34, 35, 157
Titmuss, R. N. 167

unemployment 71, 72, 83
university – *see* attainment, attainment rates and case studies, Chapter 5; awards, correlates of 144–146
urban aid programme 81, 84

Vaizey, J. 15
Valentine, C. L. 28, 160, 161
Van de Geer, J. P. 64

Wales 9
Weber, Max 32, 42
Wedderburn, D. 40
welfare capitalism 172
Welfare State, The 34
Westoby, A. and Williams, G. 40
Wigan 8, 71, 72, 83–86; attainment 86; expenditure 84–85; policy 86; provision 85–86; social-class background 83–84
Wiseman, J. P. 24

York 75
Yorkshire (West Riding) 75